The Ocean of Truth

This short book offers an alternative reading of the impact of modernity on Christian faith to that advanced by Don Cupitt in the TV series and book *The Sea of Faith*. It is a spirited defence of belief in the objective reality of God and in life after death, as opposed to Cupitt's radically interiorised and expressivist conception of religion.

As attractive as many may find a denial of the traditional doctrines of the Church in favour of an anti-metaphysical, non-dogmatic expressivist version of Christian faith, Hebblethwaite insists that of far greater importance is the question of truth at stake here, and it is on the question of truth that he focusses his attention.

After arguing against Cupitt's response to the modern situation, the author tries to show how belief in an objective God is not only possible despite the impact of modern science and historical criticism, but indeed highly plausible.

THE OCEAN OF TRUTH

A defence of objective theism

BRIAN HEBBLETHWAITE

*Fellow and Dean of Chapel in
Queens' College, Cambridge and
University Lecturer in Divinity*

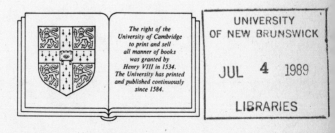

The right of the
University of Cambridge
to print and sell
all manner of books
was granted by
Henry VIII in 1534.
The University has printed
and published continuously
since 1584.

CAMBRIDGE UNIVERSITY PRESS

Cambridge
New York   New Rochelle   Melbourne   Sydney

Published by the Press Syndicate of the University of Cambridge
The Pitt Building, Trumpington Street, Cambridge CB2 1RP
32 East 57th Street, New York, NY 10022, USA
10 Stamford Road, Oakleigh, Melbourne 3166, Australia

First published 1988

Printed in Great Britain at
the University Press, Cambridge

British Library cataloguing in publication data

Hebblethwaite, Brian
The ocean of truth: a defence of
objective theism.
1. Faith
I. Title
201   BT771.2

Library of Congress cataloguing in publication data

Hebblethwaite, Brian.
The ocean of truth.
Bibliography.
Includes index.
1. Theism. 2. Apologetics – 20th century. 3. Truth
(Christian theology) 4. Cupitt, Don. I. Title.
BT102.H39   1988   231'.042   87–23914

ISBN 0 521 35182 0 hard covers
ISBN 0 521 35975 9 paperback

To myself I seem to have been only a boy playing on the seashore, and diverting myself in now and then finding a smoother pebble or a prettier shell than ordinary, while the great ocean of truth lay all undiscovered before me.

– Isaac Newton

Contents

vii

Preface

In this short book I offer an alternative reading of the impact of modernity on Christian faith to that advanced by my friend and colleague, Don Cupitt, in the television series, *The Sea of Faith*, in the book of the same title,[1] and in the five articles in 'The Listener' which accompanied the series and which are now reprinted as an appendix to Cupitt's more recent book, *Only Human*.[2] *Only Human* is the third book of a trilogy in which Cupitt has been putting forward, over the last eight years, his radically interiorised and expressivist conception of religion. The other two books are *Taking Leave of God*[3] and *The World to Come*.[4]

Cupitt's position is unusual, to say the least, in a priest of the Church of England. But there is no doubt that he speaks for many people on the fringe of the Churches, perhaps for many who would wish to think of themselves as Christians, who are still attracted by the figure of Jesus and by the Christian way, but who cannot bring themselves to assent to the traditional doctrines of the Church. To such people, an anti-metaphysical, non-dogmatic, expressivist version of Christian faith will seem attractive, even liberating. But there are questions of truth at stake here, and it is on the question of truth that I want to focus attention in my contribution to the debate.

Only in chapters two and three do I attempt a detailed discussion of Cupitt's position. I argue there against both his reading of the modern situation and his response to it. In the

ix

chapters that follow I broaden the argument, concentrating on the issues themselves, and trying to show how belief in an objective God (and in life after death) is possible, despite the impact of modern science and historical criticism – and indeed not only possible but highly plausible, given *all* the data of science, history and experience.

1

Christian belief in God

Like all the world religions, Christianity has taken and still takes many different forms. This is not only a matter of the major Church communions, Eastern Orthodox, Roman Catholic, Anglican and the numerous other Protestant denominations, with their more sectarian offshoots. Within each of these groups, Christian men and women manifest considerable differences both in belief and in practice, differences over how the Creed is understood – differences, that is, over *what* is actually believed – and differences in how the Christian way is envisaged – differences, that is, over what attitudes, practices, virtues, policies and ideals are actually enjoined. But even more basic and pervasive are the differences, again cutting across the denominations, between those Christians for whom Christianity is primarily a way of life, those for whom it is a distinctive set of cultic practices, and those for whom it is a set of very specific beliefs. These are not, of course, exclusive versions of Christianity. It is more a question of priorities. It is extremely unlikely, for instance, that Christian beliefs will be held without explicit or implicit commitment to a particular way of life. Maybe it is less unlikely that the Christian way will be embraced without assent to some at least of the beliefs of the Christian creeds. For the beliefs *can* be regarded as less important than, or as figurative or mythological expressions of, the moral and spiritual commitments that make up the Christian way. This lack of symmetry between a practice-orientated and a belief-orientated

1

understanding of Christianity – the fact that it is easier to think in terms of following the way without adhering to the doctrines than it is to affirm the doctrines without at least attempting to follow the way – might seem to tip the scales in favour of the view that Christianity is *primarily* a way of life. On the other hand, this very natural feeling for the practical priorities of the Christian religion may stem not so much from the greater importance of the way of life as opposed to the doctrines of the Creed. It may reflect the actual subject matter or content of the *beliefs* in question. The practice – and the cult – may not only follow from, but *depend* upon, the truths believed. In that case there will be something very odd about the attempt to detach the ethical and spiritual commitments from their setting in the characteristically Christian framework of belief.

Recently, in Britain, we have been confronted with a striking example of a writer and broadcaster, an academic theologian and a priest of the Church of England, who has set himself to persuade his colleagues and the public that Christianity has been misconstrued when taken to provide, even in part, a framework of belief about the ultimate nature of things. The whole aim and object of Christianity, according to Don Cupitt, is to create and provide an ideal of human life, a set of practices, disciplines and attitudes, by which we can live an authentic human life, even if we ourselves are no more than the chance products of an impersonal physical universe and destined for no more than an ordinary lifespan on the earth's surface. The language of Christianity, he holds, whether of worship or of doctrine, does not *refer* to an objective God beyond the natural world. Rather, it *expresses*, poetically, the ideal of life which Christianity commends. That is what is meant by calling this a purely 'expressivist' view. These are not new ideas. There are nineteenth-century precursors of such a radically human and subjectivist interpretation of Christianity. Already in the

2

sixties of this century we saw similar interpretations in the writings of J. H. Randall, T. R. Miles, Paul van Buren and the so-called 'death of God' theologians.[1] But such views are still unusual in an ordained Anglican theologian and the effect of their eloquent presentation on the television and in short popular articles, as well as in Cupitt's books, has been to confront the public with the possibility, even perhaps the necessity, not of a 'religionless Christianity' – in one sense, Cupitt's is a very 'religious' vision – but of a 'creedless' or 'doctrineless' Christianity, a Christianity certainly without belief in either an objective God or life after death. Moreover this understanding is presented not only as a possible interpretation or the best interpretation of the meaning of Christianity, but as the only possible one, in the light of modern scientific, philosophical and historical knowledge.

In the present chapter, I aim to contrast this proposal with what, despite the differences between communions and between believers already mentioned, I take to be the characteristic features of traditional Christian belief in God. Throughout the book, I shall refer to this traditional belief as 'objective theism', meaning thereby belief in the reality of God in an unqualified, objective sense. But clearly it will not be enough just to contrast this traditional belief with the purely expressivist version now proposed. The bulk of my reply, in subsequent chapters, will have to be devoted to showing, negatively, how an expressivist reinterpretation of Christianity is very far from being necessary, and, positively, how objective theism is quite credible and indeed most probably true, precisely in and for the modern world. If there is no alternative for religion (including Christianity) in the modern age but to adopt a purely expressivist understanding of itself, then no amount of pointing to the contrast between this view and traditional Christian belief will succeed in undermining its plausibility and force. An expressivist view undoubtedly represents a way out, if objective theism has in

3

fact become impossible in the light of modern science, philosophy and history. There would still be a question whether this is a tenable view for the Church and its commissioned ministers to adopt – this issue in contemporary ecclesiology will be considered in chapter ten and in the appendix – but the main question is whether it is a necessary view. The bulk of my reply is designed to show that other possibilities exist, moreover that objective theism is not only still possible in the modern world but actually has a great deal to be said for it. I shall argue that modernity not only permits objective theism, but in a sense requires it, if it is not itself to collapse into incoherence.

But first the contrast between the expressivist understanding of religion and traditional Christian belief in God must be brought out. We need to have before us, in more detail, what it is that is under attack and what it is that will be defended in the chapters that follow.

Not all religions are theistic. But Christianity, like Judaism and Islam, and like devotional Hinduism, Sikhism and much traditional African religion, is certainly a theistic religion. In its origins and development East and West, through the Reformation, and into its engagement with the Enlightenment and its aftermath, Christianity's Gospel of redemption, as realised in present experience and hoped for in the future, has always been preached within the horizon of belief in God – God, the infinite Creator of the world's, including our own, whole being, God, the source of all value, God, present in our midst in both incarnation and inspiration, God, who, it is believed, will in the end take his fragile personal creation, transformed, into the conditions of eternity to know and enjoy him for ever.

Christianity, so the tradition holds, has taught us to see the world as God's creation, given a definite discoverable structure and held stably in being and in God-given potency, producing out of its own God-given nature a whole world of life. It has taught us to see the human world, especially, as the sphere of God's providential activity, reaching a climax in the Incarnation of one of the personal centres of God's own eternal being within space and time and human history. This God, the source and goal of all there is, as a result of Christianity's unique experience and conception of God incarnate – and also of men and women being taken by inspiration and grace into the very life of God himself – is understood, alone among the theistic religions, in trinitarian terms. For Christianity, God is a relational, internally differentiated God, already the fulness of love given and love received, not needing to create in order to love, but nevertheless overflowing in love to new, finite, dependent creatures – ourselves.

Within this Christian theistic framework, the world around us is seen as in process, a temporary, developing phase in the creative plan, which necessarily, because of the nature of man and of the God who made him and because of the revealed and experienced relation between God and man, requires a future life beyond death in which all created persons will participate for ever and which alone will make the costly, often tragic, process of creation, burdened as it is with suffering and evil, seem worthwhile.

The significance of Jesus Christ for Christianity is inextricably bound up with Christianity's theism; for what he taught and what he achieved can only, it is held, possess the absoluteness which Christianity claims for them if they were the very words and deeds of God himself, entering the structures of creation, and living, as incarnate Son, a perfect life in relation to God the Father. It is God's own presence and closeness to us in Jesus Christ and the fate which he suffered that, according to the Christian Gospel, win our love by his great love and achieve our reconciliation. On this view it is of course God who raised Jesus from the dead and made him for ever the divine/human source and medium of our life and worship as Christians and the guarantor of our own future resurrection. The fact that Christians claim to anticipate and experience now the risen life through Christ and in the Spirit should not blind us to the fact that in the full sense resurrection to life eternal is affirmed as a future hope, only possible for Christians because of their conviction of the reality of God and of what God has done.

God, then, according to Christian understanding, in a wholly objective, realist, sense, is the source and power of the world, of history, and of our own life as creatures and children of God. It should be noted how all the facets of Christian existence – our identity, our community, our worship, our ethical ideals (both individual and social), our spirituality – are thoroughly *relational* in character. We depend on God, we are reconciled by God, we are loved by God and enabled by God to love him in return; our fellowship and our prayers are inspired and empowered by God; and it is the resources of God that both give us our ethical ideals and spiritual vision and also empower what is realised in us and through us of that vision and that ideal. And just as it is God who here and now begins to draw us into the trinitarian movement and life of God, it is God who will raise us up when we die and change and purify us for the fully realised Kingdom of God in the communion of saints in heaven.

I stress particularly how, for the Christian tradition, both ethics and spirituality are what they are and are enabled to be what they are only in relation to the God of love who inspires and enables them. This does not mean that ethics and spirituality are not found outside the horizon of Christian belief. That would be a preposterous idea. But it does mean that ethics and spirituality, wherever they are found, are believed by Christians to stem from the hidden presence and activity of God. All human goodness and all human spirituality reflect the nature and power of God.

Ethics, on a Christian understanding, is a matter not only

of our free embracing of the good, but of our being enabled to embrace the good by the grace of God working in us. Formation of character, acquisition of virtue, love in its narrower and wider senses (love, that is, of family and friends and disinterested love of the neighbour, with all its social and political implications) are understood, in Christian ethics, in terms of our responsibility before God, our being conformed to Christ, as God's Kingdom is anticipated and experienced and gradually built already this side of the divide between time and eternity. Specifically Christian ethics, then, is understood in relational terms; for the actual relation between God and man determines its source, its provisional realisations and its ultimate goal.

Spirituality, too, on a Christian understanding, is a relational matter, a growth into the dimension of God, and an ever-deepening experience of the knowledge and the love of God. Spiritual disciplines and 'exercises' are not undertaken by Christians for their own sake, as if the states of mind they produce were ends in themselves. Rather, prayer and meditation, whether alone or in the worshipping community, are believed to be the vehicles or media of exploring, enhancing and enjoying the lived relation between men and women and their Creator.

The concept of God involved in such an objective theistic understanding of the universe and man's destiny is that of an infinite, absolute, incorporeal, omnipotent, omniscient, perfectly wise and good mind or spirit. God must be thought of as infinite and absolute, if he is indeed to be both a metaphysically adequate ground and explanation of the world's being and also a religiously adequate object of worship. He must be thought of as incorporeal, since body is inherently limited and finite. He must be thought of as omnipotent and omniscient, since there is nothing outside him that could restrict his power or knowledge (except by his own will in creation – such self-limiting creation itself being

7

an exercise of omnipotence). He must be thought of as perfectly wise and good, since nothing could deflect an all-powerful, all-knowing rational will from pursuit of the best. And he must be thought of by analogy with mind or spirit, since only a creative source, endowed with will and purpose – that is, a personal source – can explain the being, nature and destiny of the world and especially of the human world.

These rationally deduced attributes of the objective God of Christian theism are echoed and complemented, so Christians hold, in the revealed attributes of the trinitarian God of love. Specifically Christian theism resolves some of the impasses of ethical monotheism by its recognition of the interpersonal nature of the source and goal of all there is and of how this God can be both transcendent and immanent, God over against us and God within. As already hinted, this trinitarian conception of God stems from experience of God incarnate and of the Spirit's indwelling. But it results in a more rationally, religiously and morally credible form of theism. Into the very life of this internally self-related deity, so Christians believe, finite creatures, men and women, are drawn and raised, both here and in eternity.

The question, of course, arises how all this can be known to be so. Traditional Christianity has offered many different answers to this question, and, as we shall see, this is one of the topics most requiring fresh examination and reform-ulation in the modern world. But in outline, it can be said that this realist, objective theism has been held to rest partly on testimony, partly on reason, and partly on experience. From another point of view, it can also be said to rest wholly on revelation. All these grounds of Christian belief will need to be discussed at greater length when we come to the impact of modernity on the tradition. Here the briefest of sketches will be offered of the way in which the tradition has spoken of the sources of faith.

Theologically speaking, Christian faith in God is understood as a response to divine revelation. General revelation is the knowledge of God made available to man through the outer and inner world in general. The reality of God is manifested to man's reason and conscience. Special revelation is the knowledge of God made available to man through a particular history and tradition reaching its climax in the life, death and resurrection of Jesus Christ. The nature and will and action of God are manifested to man's responsive faith through testimony – the testimony of Scripture and the Church to what God has done. Individual (or 'most special') revelation is the knowledge of God made available to each Christian through his or her own experience of interpreting the world and living in the world religiously and Christianly.

Revelation, then, is not one particular source among others of Christian belief in an objective God. It is rather the manifold divine activity that lies behind and is mediated through nature, conscience, history, testimony and experience. Not surprisingly, in pre-critical days, divine revelation was represented much more simplistically as a sequence of particular acts of inspiration (perhaps by a dream), of miraculous intervention in nature and history, or of verbal dictation to a human author. But we do not have to think of revelation, even in a summary account of traditional belief, in such simplistic ways. The notion of discerning the hand of God behind events and words which, from another point of view, can be described without reference to God is not a new idea. Much of what is to be found in Scripture, much traditional preaching, and much Christian theology down the ages already employ that notion.

On the other hand the idea that a completely neutral description can always be given of what Christians think of as the sources of belief in God is foreign to traditional Christianity; and indeed we shall see that it is not very plausible today. There are some rational considerations, some historical events, some testimonials, and some experiences which stand out from ordinary cases as requiring, or at least suggesting, a theistic interpretation. This will be argued from a thoroughly critical standpoint in due course. Here I simply mention some of the factors that have always weighed with Christian minds when called upon to justify belief in God.

Rational argument for the existence of God played a less central role in the ages of faith, when belief in God was part of the accepted framework in terms of which life in the world was experienced and understood. Yet the idea that the Creator is known in his handiwork and that both the natural world about us and the natural recognition of good and evil, right and wrong, point to an intelligent and moral source of all there is, is not foreign to the tradition. It takes a more philosophical form in the arguments summarised by St Thomas Aquinas in his well-known five ways.[2] They sum up, more technically, the widespread inference to God as the explanation of why there is a world at all, and as the designer of that world's hospitality to life and to personal and moral being. These considerations, as will be shown below, still have a great deal of force.

The special character of Israel's history and the religious faith that developed in conjunction with that history, and of the events surrounding the life and death of Jesus of Nazareth and their aftermath, have always been hard to explain in purely naturalistic terms. The transformation of the disciples after the crucifixion, the rapid spread of Christianity throughout the Mediterranean world and beyond, the quality of saintly lives and of the religious, including mystical, experience which Christianity has fostered and sustained, have always been cited in justification of the reality and power of God.

Human testimony to these happenings and written interpretations of what they mean – especially, of course, the testimony of Scripture – have themselves been appealed to as means of opening up the dimension of faith in the living God. Such appeals were as much to the content of Scripture and its power to convince the mind and the heart of the reality and saving grace of God as they were to the authority of Scripture as such. Indeed the latter rests on the former far more than on quasi-mechanical, pre-critical ideas of inspiration; although, hardly surprisingly, such pre-critical notions of inspiration were advanced. The role of testimony is not, of course, restricted to Scripture. The classical spiritual writings and the testimony of innumerable people in the Church down the ages, people believed to be trustworthy in their accounts of their own religious experience, have added to the weight of testimony behind the formation and defence of Christian belief in God.

The appeal to experience – one's own experience as well as that of others – had always played a crucial part in the justification of belief in God. Unless reason and testimony found confirmation in the individual believer's own experience, the faith of the Church could never have survived. In fact countless men and women down the ages – and of course not only Christian men and women – have experienced life religiously. The reality of God has manifested itself to them in wonder at the beauty of creation. The saving grace of God has been experienced where souls have turned to him in penitence and gratitude. The sustaining providential hand of God has been powerfully felt in and through and often despite the contingencies of life. Some of the most striking examples of religious experience of the reality and love of God have been in adversity and deep affliction. More commonly it is through participation in prayer and worship, and at the Blessed Sacrament of the Holy Eucharist, that Christians have, they would claim, encountered God experientially in ways that have sustained,

11

enhanced and sometimes transformed their lives as children of God. I have already mentioned how this Christian spirituality, including its ethical commitments, can only be understood in relational terms. Such religious experience, it should be noted, is not necessarily or even often a matter of being on the receiving end of bizarre miraculous occurrences. Such experience of God is usually mediated through what in themselves are quite natural instances of wonder, sorrow, gratitude, fellowship and moral or religious illumination. In particular, where the social ethical demands of Christianity are felt, God and the claims of God are believed to be encountered and experienced in the sufferings and needs of the victims of injustice and neglect.

The tradition never sought to isolate these varied kinds of religious experience, as if, by themselves, they could carry the weight of justification of Christian belief in God. Only in conjunction with the evidence of reason and testimony, it was held, could Christian appeals to experience retain their plausibility.

In this short sketch of the nature and grounds of Christian belief in God, I have tried to show how central to Christianity as a religion has been this conviction of the objective reality of God as the source and goal of all being and value. I have stressed the fact that this is so not only in respect of the central doctrines of creation, redemption and resurrection to life beyond death, but also in respect of Christian ethics and Christian spirituality. The nature and activity of God have been held to determine not only the content of ethics and spirituality, but also the realisability of Christian moral and religious ideals. Traditional Christianity has denied that man has the resources in himself to discover the full truth about his own true good, let alone actually to achieve it. Its realism about God and about the resources of God for the overcoming of evil and the attainment of the highest good is the other side of the coin from – again – its realistic recognition of man's incapacity to save himself both here in history and beyond death in eternity.

One thing about the above sketch that deserves particular note is that, neither in the outline of theistic doctrine nor in the summary of reasons for belief, have I been involved in obviously primitive or pre-critical concepts and ideas. Of course, I have to some extent deliberately suppressed such things and played down the Platonic metaphysics and Aristotelian cosmology and all elements of the blatantly miraculous and the oracular conception of Scripture that have coloured traditional belief. To do this is not to beg the question. The fact that the heart of traditional doctrine, including its indispensability for ethics and spirituality, and also the basic grounds of belief, can be set out in terms that do not necessarily commit us to first, fifth, thirteenth or sixteenth-century modes of thought is an indication of their possible transcendence of any historical and cultural setting. The question is in fact begged the other way by those who offer sketches of traditional Christianity in which the basic beliefs are inextricably tied down, for example, to the three-decker picture of the universe that characterised the thought of antiquity and the Middle Ages, or to a literal belief in miracles or in the devil. The big question to be faced in the rest of this book is whether even such an account of theistic belief as I have given can be affirmed as true in the twentieth century, given the constraints of science, historical criticism and modern philosophy. But critics make things far too easy for themselves by describing objective theism in such a way as to tie it down to obviously naive, outmoded and untenable conceptual forms.

The purpose of my sketch, given in not obviously outmoded terms, was simply to set traditional Christian theism in contrast with the subjectivist, anti-realist, expressivist view of religion and Christianity now being proposed.

In summary this view begins with the conviction that objective metaphysics, including belief in an objective God and life after death, can only be matters of idolatry and superstition in the world of modern science and philosophy. It goes on to offer, as the only possible way of positively appropriating the heart of Christianity for today, a purely voluntarist and pragmatic understanding of religion – a consistently ethical view of God as a symbol for our highest values and ideals, and of the religious life as a way of being authentically human, reinforced by and expressed in the myths, rituals and symbols of Christianity.

Well, what difference does it make if we drop the metaphysics and the doctrine and adopt this purely voluntarist, internalised and expressivist view of the Christian religion? Obviously there *is* a difference between a realist and an expressivist view of Christian discourse. There *is* a difference between an objective God and 'God' as a projected symbol of our highest ideals. There *is* a difference between believing and not believing in life after death. But, if the values and the way of life are the same, do these differences really matter? We are back with the widespread view of the priority and the sufficiency of practice mentioned at the beginning of this chapter. However, if we press and examine in detail the contrast between the traditional 'dogmatic' understanding of Christianity, with its ethics and its spirituality determined by its relation to God and the future life, and the proposed voluntarist and pragmatic view of Christianity, with its purely expressivist conception of all talk of God and eternity, we shall, I think, discover much deeper differences than simply the presence or absence of belief in an objective God. In two ways in particular does this obvious and admitted contrast affect the whole character and plausibility of Christianity as a religion.

In the first place, it becomes clear that the values and the way of life are not, after all, exactly the same whether or not we keep the metaphysics and the doctrine. It is easy to speak of a disciplined, pure life of disinterested love of one's fellow human beings as the essence of Christianity, whichever way one construes the meaning of God-talk and eternity-talk. Forgiveness, reconciliation, peace and justice sound much the same when advanced as ideals of life by theists and non-theists alike. But in fact these qualities and ideals of life turn out rather differently when they are experienced and embraced as effects of gratitude, grace and the divine indwelling. When they flow not just from the will as purely human products, but from a real relation to the personal ground of our being, they cannot be thought of as identical with humanist values, for all the latter's worth. To take but one example, the love apostrophised by St Paul in I Corinthians 13 is not the bare affirmation of disinterested concern. Where the other is seen as a child of God, and where human interpersonal relation is believed to find its own true fulfilment in conformity to and inspiration by the inner-trinitarian love of the God who made us, love occurs in a different dimension and takes on other transcendent qualities. The love of Mother Teresa of Calcutta for the poor and destitute is demonstrably different from that of the secular relief worker – with no disparagement to the latter. Similarly, the belief in life beyond death and the hope for an eventual realised consummation of the Kingdom of God in heaven are bound to alter the tone of men's values and ideals. Admittedly they can affect people's commitments adversely, deflecting energies and concerns from immediate tasks – but only when misconstrued. For, properly understood and actually experienced, the love of God and the hope of heaven inspire a sustained and self-critical commitment to the realisation of the Kingdom that neither gives up when frustrated, nor confuses the possible with the impossible here on earth.

This leads to the second way in which the contrast between theistic and non-theistic ways of understanding Christianity affects the character and plausibility of the religion. Not only do the values and ideals turn out be subtly and profoundly different in the context of a real, relational, conception of God and eternity, but the whole question of their practical realisability is different. Men need the resources of God's indwelling grace and inspiration if these values and ideals are to be realised humanely. A voluntarist, purely expressivist view of Christianity might possibly work, to some extent at least, in occasional cases. But the majority of people need a power not themselves that makes for righteousness, that converts and sustains and builds up not only individuals but groups of men and women in the Church. One aspect of this practical difference which the reality of God makes to the realisation of the Kingdom will be touched on in chapter ten, when I ask how far a voluntarist, expressivist view could be expected to sustain a Church or a world religion. My immediate point is to question whether the individual has it in him to change and develop in the direction of the Christian ideal, with no help other than that of his fellow Christians.

I suggest, therefore, that the contrast between a realist and an expressivist view of Christianity is very great. Moreover it is a contrast that matters. The Church can hardly be expected to abandon without a struggle its central conviction that the character and power of the Christian way *depend* on the reality of God.

2
The ebbing of theistic faith

The nature of objective theism and its centrality for historical Christianity have been set out briefly in chapter one. But even when sketched sympathetically in not obviously outmoded terms, such theism, it must be acknowledged, has come under increasing strain since the Enlightenment and the rise of modern science. In the context of modern western civilisation and in areas increasingly permeated by western culture, it is not easy to retain and live within the theistic framework presupposed and taught by all the Christian churches. The decreasing hold of such belief in God on popular consciousness as well as on the intelligentsia has been documented and studied by many cultural historians and sociologists. Admittedly, this process of secularisation is by no means universal nor uniform. There is still a great deal of religion, including belief in God, to be found in today's world. There is also a great deal of interest in mysticism and the occult. Popular superstititions thrive. Nor are the reasons or causes for the widespread phenomenon of secularisation by any means all rational. We shall consider in this chapter both reasons and causes for the ebbing of theistic faith. I say nothing of the deliberate attempt in communist countries to suppress belief. A case can be made for thinking that policy to be less successful in eradicating belief in an objective God than are the non-coercive factors operative in western liberal societies.

Despite the considerable evidence that exists for the continued vitality of theism among the variegated manifestations of contemporary religion, I accept the overall picture of secularisation and an ebbing of theistic faith in modern western civilisation as a fact and proceed now to examine both the reasons and the causes of this. I shall concentrate attention on the reasons, as Cupitt does in his telling presentation of some of the key factors and figures behind the making of the modern world. But even where the reasons for the erosion of belief in God are concerned, it will be important to distinguish their valid from their invalid scope and application. It will become clear that the impact of the discoveries of figures such as Galileo, Darwin, Freud, Strauss, Marx and Nietzsche has not been entirely a rational impact. In many aspects of modernity, it will be argued, rational considerations have been pushed to irrational extremes, with non-rational factors conspiring to create a world view that has no place for an objective God. In fact, my strategy is much the same as Cupitt's; for he too rejects the positivist, materialist conclusions to which the secularisation process has led. But whereas he attempts to recover the religious dimension internally by an interiorisation of ethical and spiritual values which he holds to be essentially untouched by modern science, I attempt to show that theistic metaphysics no more than ethics is an inevitable casualty of modernity. I attempt to show as well that it is not so easy to detach ethics and spirituality from metaphysics in the context of modern thought.

The figure of Galileo, the seventeenth-century astronomer, whose proof that the earth revolved around the sun was rejected vehemently by the Church of his day, symbolises well the immense shock given by the rise of modern science to the medieval picture of the world, inherited from antiquity, with which traditional Christian beliefs had inevitably come to be

18

associated. It is easy to portray Galileo, as Bertolt Brecht portrayed him in his play of the same name, as a symbol of enlightenment against prejudice and superstition; and certainly the story of his enforced recantation is a tragic and shameful human story. But the shame of the early seventeenth-century Church has little to do with the question whether Christian belief in a creator God is inextricably bound up with Aristotelian cosmology and a static geo-centric picture of the universe. No one now denies that Galileo was right and the Church which condemned him was wrong.

It is perfectly true that for Christian theology to accept and welcome modern cosmology, it has not only to free itself from its historically determined links with Aristotle and Ptolemy but also to free itself from certain over-literal ways of reading its own Scriptures. The Scriptures are, of course, more central to historical Christianity's self-understanding than are Aristotle and Ptolemy. But the creation myths of Genesis and the poetic language of prophecy and psalm, in which the dependence of the whole world on God for its being and order are most vividly expressed, do not in any way entail the rejection of Copernicus and Galileo, nor indeed of Newton and Einstein. Figurative, pictorial representations of the dependence relation between the world and God are quite compatible with modern cosmology. Indeed the Christian doctrine of creation itself desacralises the world and sets it free for empirical investigation and for scientific theorising and experiment. Christian theology is well placed to acknowledge and welcome the autonomous domain of scientific enquiry into the elements, structures, laws and processes of the physical universe.

Nor does Christianity's insistence on the value and significance of man depend on a geocentric picture of the universe. We shall see in later chapters how modern cosmology in fact enhances the centrality of man as it

discloses the precision and 'fine tuning' of the initial conditions making possible the emergence of life and mind at a
later stage in cosmic evolution.[1] On any view, the capacity
of this vast expanding universe to come up with the conditions
that make for life and personal being on earth is a fact to
excite great wonder.

If there was a threat in Galileo's work for a Christian
conception of the world, it lay not in the subjection of the
physical universe to scientific study nor in the abandonment
of the Ptolemaic geocentric view. It was, as Cupitt shows,[2]
the implications of a mechanical universe for traditional ideas
of prayer and providence that were to be felt more seriously
to undermine the Christian faith. But it is important to realise
that prayer and providence would not be the only casualties
of a universal application of mechanism. If mechanical
models, appropriate enough to galaxies and stars and planetary systems, are applied to every aspect of man's life on
earth, then rigid determinism follows; and not only prayer
and providence but free will, ethics and creativity are
threatened too. Now Cupitt himself rejects the mechanical
model of the universe at this point. He traces a path of
interiorisation, whereby the human being, product of a
mechanical universe though he be, comes to transcend it
ethically and religiously by his will and creativity. This
voluntarist, pragmatic view itself requires the refutation of
determinism where man is concerned. But if ethics and
creativity can be rescued from the implications of a mechanical universe, why not prayer and providence? Indeed the
tables can be turned. Without a theology of providence, it is
hard to see the rationale behind an affirmation of free will.
The ways in which man escapes the deterministic causal grid
are much more of a mystery on a naturalistic than on a
creationist view of the world.

These problems will be considered further in subsequent
chapters. At this point, we have simply located the main

problem for Christianity of the mechanical universe disclosed by Galileo. But we have also seen that it is not only a problem for Christian theology. Any moral and creative view of man has to reckon with human transcendence in an apparently deterministic world. The problems of divine transcendence are no less difficult, but no more insoluble, than those of human transcendence; and in fact, as we shall see, much thought has gone into working out theories of divine providence in relation to a scientific understanding of causality. Clearly a doctrine of providence will require some limitation of the scope of the mechanistic theory; but morality and art require that too.

The pattern of innovation, excessive reaction and necessary but critical reassessment that we have noticed in the case of Galileo repeats itself in that of Darwin. Of all the makers of the modern world, Darwin has had the greatest effect on attitudes to religion and Christianity, at both the intellectual and the popular level, in western civilisation. Church reaction against the theory of evolution was a much more natural and intelligible affair than Church reaction again the Copernican revolution in astronomy. The idea that man had evolved by natural selection from the animal world seemed to strike at the roots of religion and morality. It gravely damaged the argument for design and appeared to supply a purely naturalistic alternative to the biblical portrayal of the special creation of man in the image of God. The significance of man in the world appeared to be much more gravely threatened by his being rooted in the natural animal world than by his losing merely physical centrality in the cosmos. Moreover belief in the special creation of man by God was a more central biblical idea than was geocentric cosmology. The theory of evolution is still resisted by fundamentalists in a way in which Copernican, Newtonian or Einsteinian cosmology is not.

Yet the mainstream Churches and their theologians have long since come to accept evolutionary theory as entirely compatible with the Christian doctrine of creation. There may still be some doubts – on the part of biologists and theologians alike – about its adequacy, even in its post-Mendelian form, as a complete explanatory account of the emergence and evolution of species up to man.[3] But its broad parameters are accepted and the necessary adjustments to theological understanding have been made. It is acknowledged that evolution through natural selection constitutes God's mode of gradual, continuous creation. The Genesis stories are recognised as mythological portrayals of the world's and man's dependence on the Creator; and the story of the fall is reinterpreted, non-historically, as portraying the distance between man and God, whereby all human beings fall short of the ideal God-man relationship which is their destiny in the divine intention. Such reformulations of the doctrines of creation and fall, in the light of evolutionary theory, also affect a Christian understanding of providence. The manner in which the Creator, without disrupting the natural story, brings it about that cosmic (not just biological) evolution leads to the emergence of personal creatures who can come to know and love their Maker, becomes paradigmatic for the understanding of God's action in the world. In the words of Austin Farrer, 'God makes the creature make itself'.[4]

These reformulations of the Christian understanding of creation, fall and providence are by no means tactical retreats in face of unpalatable but undeniable discoveries. Christians have learned not only to distinguish between biblical myths and the truths those myths express, but also to think out much more profoundly and coherently the relation between the underlying 'primary' causality of God and the God-given 'secondary' causality of creatures. Moreover, acceptance of an evolutionary picture of the cosmos and the life, has enabled new forms of the design argument to arise from the ashes of the old. The very fact of the universe's capacity to evolve not only living but rational and personal beings itself becomes an indication of intelligent design, as we shall see.[5]

There remain two major negative legacies of Darwin, which perhaps go further to explain his continuing erosive effect on a theistic view of the world. One concerns the problem of evil, the other the possibility of a purely natural, biological theory of the development of morality and religion themselves. It is often felt that if natural selection is the indirect method through which providence gradually fashions a world of life, it is much too wasteful a process, prodigal of suffering and pain, to attribute to a benevolent divine will. In fact the problem of evil is no greater (and no less) whether or not we accept the theory of evolution. Its resolution is a task imperative on any kind of realistic theism. Without pursuing the matter in detail here, we may suggest that if the point of God's gradual creation in and through an evolving world of life can be appreciated − it may be that rooting man thus in a regular, self-reproducing and self-balancing, ecological system is *necessary* to the creative purpose − then the problem of evil may be eased rather than increased by the integration of a Darwinian view into the doctrines of creation and providence.

The other problem is rather different. As Cupitt shows,[6] there is a hint here of the extension of biology into the mental, the moral, the social and the religious, bringing all within the scope of a naturalistic reductive theory. But, as with the universal application of the mechanistic view, this extension has to be questioned and criticised not only by the theist, but also by the moralist. At this point too, human life itself, not just theistic religion, transcends its naturalistic base. If Cupitt's radically interiorised faith can resist the inroads of sociobiology, so too can belief in divine providence and grace.

The effect of Freud's work on religious belief in an objective God is more direct and damaging than that of Galileo or Darwin. Belief in God is here subjected to assault rather than to erosion. Moreover Freud's objections to religion are moral as well as intellectual. On the other hand, Freud is a much more controversial figure than Galileo or Darwin. There is much less of incontrovertible validity to be received from his work. This is true not only of his treatment of religion, but also of his psychoanalytic work in general. Admittedly, we have learned to think differently and more realistically about the unconscious factors motivating our thought and action. Even if we reject the ubiquity of repressed sexual motivation, it is undeniable that we think differently about sex since Freud. If our view of other people and ourselves is more pessimistic, it is also perhaps more charitable, and we have learned to reckon with the underlying dynamics of personal and interpersonal existence. But, as Cupitt himself points out,[7] Freud has remarkably little to say about the more positive, creative and rational sides of human life. Where religion is concerned, Cupitt makes this point in favour of his own affirmation of critical, creative, religious values. What we must also ask is whether Jewish and Christian belief in an objective God is as vulnerable to Freud's intellectual and moral objections as Cupitt happily assumes.

Freud's moral objections to objective theism are far more powerful than his intellectual ones. Indeed the intellectual objections are remarkably thin. He simply assumed atheism, ignoring the rational arguments for the existence of God which constitute the subject matter of 'natural theology', and offering the most implausible account of the origin of theism in the childhood of the human race. Much more powerful is his evident moral sense that the projection of a father-figure on to the heavens represents an infantile stage in human development, evident in the neurotic symptoms of obsessive ritual behaviour. The force of Freud's objection to theism is felt wherever religious belief and practice have had something of these characteristics. Clearly religion is its own worst enemy where it invites portrayal in these terms.

But the moral and intellectual plausibility of religious belief in God must be assessed at its best, not at its worst. Intellectually speaking, there is a case, as we shall see,[8] for holding that both the scientific and the human worlds require us to postulate an infinite creative mind and will as their first cause, if they are to be intelligible at all. Morally speaking, there is plenty of evidence from the lives of innumerable men and women of faith (in Christianity and other religions) to show that belief in God, far from inhibiting freedom and maturity, enables human life to be lived more creatively, more profoundly, more *freely*, as people discover that their true freedom lies in the spontaneity of unrestricted and undistorted love. Of course, Freud was not the only post-Enlightenment thinker to assume that an objective God must be an overpowering alienating force. Already the early Hegel had pressed this accusation against what he took to be the dominant Jewish and Christian conceptions of God.[9] Hegel himself already saw that the answer to this moral objection lay in the idea of God as the spirit of love, inspiring love from within the human heart and the human community. Freud is to be answered in the same way. God is not the projection of an angry father-figure. He is both the source of and the resource for authentic human freedom and love. Precisely as such, however, he must be real, not just ideal. The discovery of theistic religion is that freedom and love are not mere human inventions, but are made possible and sustained in unlooked for ways by the gracious presence and power of the Creator of all things.

The figure of the radical, nineteenth-century biblical critic, David Friedrich Strauss, is much less well known than those of Galileo, Darwin or Freud. But his importance for our study of the reasons for the ebbing of theistic faith in modern times is equally great, if less general in its scope. The name of Strauss is cited in connection with the apparently destructive effect of the application of the historical critical method to the Jewish and Christian Scriptures. So here we are concerned, not with the impact of the Enlightenment on our whole understanding of the cosmos and of life, but with its impact on the Bible and our understanding of revelation. But the pattern is similar to that which we observed in the cases of Galileo and Darwin. It is again a question of distinguishing the valid from the invalid, the necessary and incontrovertible innovations from the excessive and extreme conclusions, drawn in this case by Strauss himself.

The problem may be put, very simply, like this. The Bible, traditionally, was seen as the book of the acts of God. Its subject matter is what God has done, is doing and will do. It abounds, as other religious scriptures do, with tales of the supernatural, the miraculous, and the other-worldly. The Bible itself had taken on something of the character of the supernatural – in its alleged divine inspiration and infallibility. Historical criticism, however, shows that the Bible, like all other scriptures and religious books, is a natural, fallible, all-too-human product, the repository of many different men and women's religious experiences and expectations. The erosion of the Bible's divine status contributes to the erosion of belief in miracles and providence, including the Incarnation and resurrection, and ultimately to the erosion of belief in God.

To put the matter like this shows up the lack of nuance and discrimination in popular conceptions both of traditional views of the Bible and of post-critical reactions to the discovery of its human, historically-conditioned character. For it is quite clear that Christian faith in an objective God does not stand or fall with a literalist, fundamentalist conception of Scripture. We have already mentioned the ways in which the

Genesis myths of creation and fall can be seen as figurative representations of the total dependence of the world on God and of the distance between man and God that needs to be overcome. Similarly, in the light of critical historical study into the ways in which the faith of Israel developed and into the biblical witness to the events which gave birth to Christianity, Christian theology learns to think more carefully and more profoundly about the way God works in the world in and through the history of a particular people's self-understanding, to fashion a context in which he can reveal his nature, purpose and will. Such a theology will learn to distinguish between miracle and providence and will tend to see the former as a figurative representation of the latter. Its understanding of the Incarnation will be much more subtle than in terms of miraculous intervention, though it will still be interventionist in a more serious sense. It will realise, for example, that God's presence and action in our midst in an incarnate human life do not necessarily depend on a virginal conception. Only the resurrection – that unique anticipation of the expected destiny of all – will escape the possibility of articulation in terms of providence, that is, in terms of *mediated* divine action in and through an apparently natural human story. But it will seek to show both historical and experiential reasons for postulating something unique at that point. It will also seek to show such reasons for postulating more than a naturalistic account of the origins and nature of Christianity as a whole.

It should not surprise us that the first attempts to give a historically and critically informed account of the Christian Scriptures should have been taken to destructive extremes. It took time and much hard work before the acts of God in creation, providence, incarnation, redemption and grace were thought through in ways which respected both the natural and historical media of divine revelation and the thoroughly human character of the biblical witness to that revelation. But it is not only the fact that such historically and theologically informed interpretations are possible that disproves the view that there is no alternative to a purely voluntarist, expressivist analysis of the language of the Bible. It is also the fact that such theologically realist interpretations are required by the evidence, taken as a whole, even when subjected to the canons of the historical critical method. The argument of this book is, in part, that the history of religions (in particular the history of Israel) and also the circumstances giving rise to Christianity, cannot satisfactorily be understood except in terms of divine action and divine revelation. To press this point at the most central, if also the most difficult instance, the 'appearances' tradition, the 'empty tomb' tradition, the rapid and radical transformation of the dejected apostles into dynamic leaders of a new universalistic religion, and the subsequent religious experiences of the Christians, are only intelligible on the supposition of the resurrection of Jesus Christ from the dead.

Such a reading of the evidence, it will be objected, presupposes belief in an objective God. That belief was indeed basic to the whole thought-world of biblical, patristic and medieval man. But in the modern world, it is essential to realise that the case for objective theism does not rest solely on biblical evidence. There are other reasons too for adopting the theistic framework which makes the above reading of the historical evidence most plausible. It is precisely in the wake of post-Enlightenment scepticism that we need to draw attention to those reasons if the historical evidence, duly sifted, is to carry its proper weight.

The impact of Karl Marx on the modern world has been very great and, as with Freud, his assault on religion was specific and direct. As pointed out above, that assault has been institutionalised in the attempts of most communist countries to eradicate religion. But I concentrate here on the intellectual and moral objections to belief in God which Marx and Marxism have encouraged throughout the world. Once again, intellectual fashion rather than argument lies behind Marx's unquestioning assumption that it was right to reduce theology to anthropology and to see the idea of God as a projection of ideal humanity. Marx sharpened the critique by treating this illusory projection as an alienating factor, offering false solace to an oppressed humanity. But this brings us to the moral objection. Marx's moral objection to objective theism was even more devastating and important than was Freud's. Marx came to believe that the necessary social revolution would entail the abolition of religion just because belief in God, on the part of oppressed and oppressors alike, fixates social relationships in their alienated, pre-revolutionary forms. There is plenty of evidence to show that the Christian religion has played this role at times in history, and once again the force of this objection is felt wherever religious belief and practice have actually had these characteristics. One need only think of the notorious verse in Mrs Alexander's hymn 'The rich man in his castle, the poor man at his gate. God made them high and lowly, and ordered their estate'.

But it is quite clear that theistic religion need not have these morally objectionable social effects. Once again we should reckon both with the rational and religious case for belief in God and with the fact (and therefore the possibility) of more authentic forms of theistic faith which, from Old Testament times on, have inspired the quest for social justice. The very fact that Marx and Marxism themselves, with varying degrees of plausibility, can be called upon to illuminate and aid such forms of Christian social ethics as Latin American 'Liberation Theology' shows that the Christian God can be – and many would say must be – thought of as the One who sets free, not only internally through redemption from personal bondage of the will, but also politically through an inspired corporate commitment to a just, participatory and sustainable society.

I have deliberately used the terminology here of the social – ethical teaching of the World Council of Churches rather than that of Marx himself, because at this point the tables must be turned on the Marxist critique and strong moral objections levelled at its undoubtedly Promethean character. Part of the moral case for theism is the widespread sense, for which historical evidence has been accumulating at a terrible pace in the twentieth century, that the idea that man can create his own future – for Marx that means socialism – by his own effort is itself deeply flawed and self-destructive. The secular mind is already aware of this, as it contemplates with horror the cost which Promethean man is prepared to exact from his fellow men in order to construct an allegedly ideal society. But secular man's appeal to the cause of human rights in face of Marxist (and other) tyranny is insecurely based. Religion itself can be a source of tyranny, but it can also be a source of self-critical inspiration as, under God, responsibly and with humility, men let themselves become the instruments of God's reconciling and unifying purpose. Once again we may affirm that men and women need a power *not themselves* that makes for righteousness. It can be argued too that the only proper basis for a commitment to human rights is recognition of each human person as a child of God.

The sheer ambiguity of the trends and tendencies that have shaped the modern world comes clearly into view when we turn to the all too Promethean figure of the nineteenth-century prophet of 'the death of God', Friedrich Nietzsche. In no way can the writings of Nietzsche be thought of as supplying a reason for, or even a cause of, the ebbing of theistic faith. He is much too bizarre and irrational a figure to be accorded such an influential status. But he certainly takes atheism to its logical conclusion, and expresses and exemplifies, dramatically, the nature and effect of man without God. Hence his interest to theologians such as Karl Barth, who was able to show us how to learn from what is diametrically opposed to Christianity something of the true nature of Christian realism, Christian faith in a God of love, and a Christian ethic of an other-directed love.[10] Nietzsche is unquestionably opposed to everything held by Christianity to be true and good and it is quite extraordinary that some modern Christians have tried to elevate him into a reformer, clearing the way for a purified Christianity.[11] In fact even his most attractive ideas, for example his powerful affirmation of life, turn out to be thoroughly egoistic and cruel and, not surprisingly, self-destructive.

Nietzsche's ethic of self-assertion corresponds to his conviction of the death of God and his thoroughgoing nihilism. It is, of course, quite impossible to take the idea of the death of God literally. It can only refer to the death of *belief* in God as a basic element in modern consciousness. But the importance of Nietzsche lies in his showing how pervasive is the effect of this loss of faith. Nothing remains the same. Not only do traditional moral values crumble. Reality and truth, as well, are evaporated away. Not only God, but an independent, ordered external world, to say nothing of a given human nature, dissolve. In Nietzsche's own words, 'truth is fiction', and nothing remains but sheer Promethean self-assertion and will.

The reason why Cupitt takes this universal nihilism as a possible starting point for his reconstruction of Christianity on a purely voluntarist basis[12] is that such ungrounded creativity does not have to be egoistic. If anything is possible, disinterestedness is possible, and that is what Cupitt recommends as the project for any future Christianity. In theory, such a purely human ethic and spirituality could be envisaged as being erected over a Nietzschean void. But there are a number of factors which make this a highly implausible suggestion. In the first place, it shows how far one has to go if ethics and spirituality are to be prized apart from any grounding in reality and truth. On this view, our whole world, not just our system of values, is a purely human invention. And to suggest that we should go all the way with Nietzsche in order to clear the ground for the total construction of our world as well as of our values is not likely to persuade anyone who retains some sense for reality and truth even in everyday affairs and scientific enquiry. In a later chapter it will be argued that our ordinary conviction that the world, including human life, is what it is and not a creation of our own but something given, enables us to resist Nietzschean fantasy and indeed provides a starting point for an argument from truth to God.[13] Secondly, the sheerly Promethean nature of the project of lifting ourselves up, ethically and spiritually, by our own boot-straps stands out all the more clearly in this Nietzschean context. It is highly implausible to suggest that Christianity could ever be thought of in these terms. Nietzsche himself was surely right to hold that Christianity's identity is bound up with ideas of dependence, response, and a spiritual resource not our own. Thirdly, it seems highly unlikely that a Church, still less a world religion, could be constructed and maintained on this basis. This objection will be pursued further in chapter ten. The example of Buddhism, which indeed comes closest to such an anti-metaphysical, pragmatic religious project, will be considered in chapter eight.

There are many other factors than those associated with the names of Galileo, Darwin, Freud, Strauss, Marx and Nietzsche, that have contributed to the secularisation of the modern western mind and to the ebbing of theistic faith. Major changes in society and in social relationships, through industrialisation, urbanisation, the proliferation of modern technology and the growth of consumer-orientated economies have accelerated the tendency to think of man as a product of nature now come of age and capable of constructing his own future in purely this-worldly terms. But the deepest sources of modern man's loss of theistic faith are undoubtedly the factors we have been considering, a mechanistic view of the universe, a naturalistic conception of man himself, a purely historical view of religion and the Bible, and a psychologically and socially based moral critique of the nature and effects of belief in God.

In this chapter we have seen that, where modern cosmology and evolutionary theory are concerned, incontrovertible discoveries have been made and a new perspective opened up that religion and theology cannot possibly deny or ignore. There is also no denying the great changes that have taken place in Christian self-understanding through acceptance of a historical and critical approach to the Bible and to the development of Christian doctrine. Moreover, where forms of theistic faith have been infected by and frozen into psychologically immature behaviour patterns and socially unjust structures and relations, moral criticism is not only valid but imperative.

But we have also seen that objective theism is quite capable of taking account of these advances in knowledge and indeed of developing a more coherent and profound conception of the divine creative and providential activity in and through an ordered world whose basic structures can be explored in the natural and the human sciences. Furthermore, it is not only Christian theism that places a limit on the mechanistic and biologistic models with which the sciences operate. Human personality, including responsibility and freedom, human interpersonal relationships culminating in altruism and love, human creativity in art, and human spirituality themselves all transcend the causal grid of their physical, chemical and biological base, before ever the question of divine transcendence and activity is raised. The same point has been made about the much more controversial forms of psychological and social determinism that have characterised the extension of scientific method from the natural into the human worlds. The idea that any of these discoveries, the more secure cosmological and biological ones, or the less secure psychological and sociological ones, make belief in an objective God impossible for modern man has been shown to be quite unsubstantiated. I have yet to make the positive case for holding that the universe disclosed to modern science suggests or *requires* such theism.

This chapter has also indicated briefly how recognition of the historical nature of the Christian religion, its Scriptures and its doctrines, represents no threat to objective theism. On the contrary, theistic faith becomes a less naive and more profound possibility once Christians learn to appreciate the fallible and developing media through which God acts and reveals himself. But again, the possibility of reconciling theistic faith with a critical historical approach to the Bible is only half the story. It will be argued in subsequent chapters that a critically liberated, biblical faith in God is actually needed in the modern world. It has also been suggested here that moral objections to objective theism must be taken seriously, albeit with discrimination. Only a false idea of God oppresses. There is no necessary connection between the reality of God and psychological immaturity or social conservatism. On the contrary, Christian faith in a trinitarian God, who liberates by self-sacrificial love and inspires by uncoercive indwelling, should lead to mature self-discovery and realistic self-critical commitment to the doing of God's will, which in any case, according to Christianity, prescribes man's own true good.

It may well be thought that psychological immaturity (and excessive individualism) are much more characteristic of the inflated and ultimately self-destructive Prometheanism of Nietzsche. There is in Nietzsche and his followers a kind of adolescent delight in kicking over the traces and an illusory demand for absolute autonomy. Responsible moral and spiritual life requires, rather, a proper recognition of both freedom and dependence.

3

The interiorisation of faith

The argument of the last chapter was that the various factors which have gone into the making of our modern scientific and critical consciousness, although entailing considerable revision and reformulation of traditional Christian theism, in no way require the abandonment of theistic metaphysics altogether. It is simply not true to say that there is no alternative to a purely interiorised and expressivist understanding of religious language.

In this chapter I turn to an examination of Cupitt's 'interiorisation' thesis itself. So far I have characterised it by means of a string of adjectives, mostly taken from Cupitt's writings: subjectivist, anti-metaphysical, non-dogmatic, expressivist, voluntarist, pragmatic, internalised or interiorised. Each of these must now be considered in some detail.

The sense in which this position must be deemed *subjectivist* is clear. On this view, religion is entirely a product of human subjects. It is not evoked by a response to objective metaphysical realities – in particular the reality of God – over against the human subject. It is not a relational phenomenon, depending on and articulating a real relation between believers and their God. It is rather a matter of purely human ideas, disciplines and aspirations. Of course it is not 'subjective' in a purely inward private sense. It is a collective, inter-subjective phenomenon. And it certainly gets expressed in rituals and institutions, which themselves acquire a solidly objective quality in the world. But, for all that, there are no objective values; there is no objective life after death and no objective God. So it is not unreasonable to call this view 'subjectivist'. But as we shall see throughout this chapter, Cupitt is able to trade on a pervasive ambiguity concerning the way in which the human subject is indeed the primary vehicle of knowledge of God. The inward journey of intense subjectivity has, from the time of St Augustine, been recognised to be the principal mode of access to spiritual realities. But it is one thing to hold that God is first and foremost encountered in the 'cave of the heart', quite another to hold that 'God' is a name for the heart's own highest aspirations and ideals. My criticism of this subjectivist understanding of religion is threefold. It fails to recognise the need to postulate an objective source and goal of all there is. It is blind to the revelation from beyond which comes to expression in the history of religions and in that to which the Bible bears witness. And it fails to supply the power and resources for life 'in the Spirit', which only an objective God can give.

The position under consideration is certainly *anti-metaphysical*. Metaphysics is the name given, since Aristotle, to those very general questions of meaning, truth and being which arise beyond the specific subject matters of the natural and human sciences when we ask about the origin, explanation, meaning and destiny of the world and of human life. Cupitt seems to accept without any qualms the views of empiricists, even positivists, who declare (without much argumentation) that such questions are unanswerable or even unaskable. In fact this hard-line positivism – and indeed empiricism itself – has been subjected to very penetrating criticism in modern philosophy; and, although the enterprise of metaphysics is still a highly controversial one, there are many forms of metaphysical thinking current and influential in both science and philosophy today. Some of these current metaphysical theistic possibilities will be discussed in the next chapter. The fact is that these basic 'why' questions – why are the laws and energies and structures of the universe what they are? – why have they the capacity to produce living and rational beings? – what is the meaning of human life? – these basic questions will not go away. In particular it is deeply counter-intuitive to suggest that religion of all things should not be interested in such questions. Certainly there are other important questions with which religion is also much concerned. What sort of person should I be? What is to be done? How can I contribute to making the world a better place? But the vast majority of religious people, past and present, have seen the two sorts of question, theoretical and practical, as inextricably linked. Indeed most religions hold that answers to the practical questions in the end *depend* on answers to the theoretical ones. Religion is deeply involved with metaphysics. It presupposes, depends on and implies beliefs which can only be categorised as metaphysical. An anti-metaphysical conception of religion is, therefore, responding to and expressing only a fraction of man's religious sense. Moreover, a blanket opposition to metaphysics renders that remaining fragment of religion wholly unintelligible. It is not just that the religious values thus espoused seem arbitrary; man's capacity to espouse them, if he is no more than the product of blind forces, is quite inexplicable. So there is a deep incoherence in an anti-metaphysical conception of religious value.

At this point I will interpose a comment on the folly of more traditional theological opposition to metaphysics. Whether one thinks of Tertullian, Luther, Kierkegaard or Karl Barth, one is struck how easily theological hostility to metaphysics and philosophy backfires. The religious motivation behind such attempts to detach faith from speculation and turn the heart away from the abstract God of the philosophers to the living God of Abraham, Isaac and Jacob is quite understandable, but it plays straight into the hands of subjectivist critics of realist theology. I submit, therefore, that a religious faith in God has metaphysical implications which it is in no way irreligious to try to spell out. To consider the philosophical aspects of belief in God is not to resort to an abstract God; it is rather to abstract, for theoretical consideration, certain presuppositions of faith in the living God. That this is not only legitimate but necessary is shown by the vulnerability of a faith that despises philosophy to purely subjectivist and expressivist analyses of all religious language.

Cupitt's position is also *non-dogmatic* in that he pleads explicitly for religion without dogma. So not only are metaphysical speculations rejected but also Church dogmas, in any realist, objective sense. The word 'dogma' has certain overtones which may deprive its real meaning of sympathy in those not otherwise hostile to belief in an objective God. 'Dogmatic' has connotations of prejudice and a refusal to listen to reason. But these connotations are quite irrelevant to the point at issue. For purely voluntarist and interiorised conceptions of the Christian faith are equally opposed to doctrines and beliefs, however openly, critically and rationally considered they may be. Such a view rejects dogma in the much more far-reaching and thoroughgoing sense of entirely rejecting *factual* belief in God and in life after death as being wholly mistaken and not an integral part of religion at all. This brings us back to the double theme of my response – to the question whether religious faith essentially involves the assertion of fact about matters transcending the empirical world, and to the question whether such fact-asserting, transcendental beliefs are possible in the modern world. The reason for answering both questions in the affirmative are: firstly, without the truth of doctrine Christianity loses both its identity and its power; and secondly, sufficient reasons have not been given either to disprove the possibility of theistic faith or to rebut the arguments in its favour.[1]

The view of Christianity advanced by Cupitt is an *expressivist* view in that it treats all religious language, including talk of God and of eternity, as expressive of ideas and commitments and ways of life held to constitute not only the essence but the whole of the religion in question. The Christian cult – its liturgies, sacraments and prayers – are also all expressive of its ideal and its way. Such an analysis holds some attraction for the religious mind; for it can be put in religiously profound and telling ways, and of course it encapsulates a partial truth about religion. Furthermore, it can trade on the religiously unappealing abstract character of much of the typical argumentation to be found in theologically realist philosophy of religion such as that of Alvin Plantinga or Richard Swinburne.[2]

The partial truth in this view lies in the fact that religious language and ritual are indeed highly expressive modes of discourse and action. Consider the cases of psalmody and hymnody – both of them being religiously evocative, poetical modes of expression. But the question arises *what* it is that they express. A fair reply, from a phenomenological as well as from a philosophical point of view, is that they do not only express commitments and ideals – though of course they do express these things – but they also express such things as gratitude to God, the love of God, and hope for the future, both here and in eternity. So the reply to a purely expressivist analysis must take the twofold form of showing how the factual beliefs, abstracted by philosophers for theoretical consideration, are themselves integral to and evocative of highly religious attitudes, commitments and ideals. Correlatively, it has to be shown how these commitments and ideals, for all their moral and religious force, are likely to evaporate and dissolve away if deprived of their factual basis. A purely expressivist view of religion is incoherent in the sense that it lacks the only context that can realistically be supposed capable of sustaining religious values in the world.

This is at the same time to argue against a purely *voluntarist* conception of religious faith. No doubt the will does play a crucial role in any religious approach to life. Man's freedom to make or mar his world, his responsibility for what he does and for what he makes of his life, are important religious themes. So are the limitations on man's freedom that make him incapable of bringing about his own salvation by his own effort. This is not the place to rehearse the case for the key place of free will in theodicy or the arguments, classically advanced by Luther and Erasmus, over the scope of man's bondage or freedom. But Erasmus no more than Luther would have countenanced the suggestion that Christianity itself, its values and its ideal are a pure creation of the human will, that grace is a metaphor for a freely espoused quality of life, and that God is a personification of the religious ideal, freely projected by human subjects. The Gospel must indeed be freely embraced by those who hear its claim. But what they embrace is a resource not their own that breaks the bondage of the will and sets the human subject free to live and share the Christian life in the power of the Spirit.

A man's will is not suppressed or overborne in this process. What looks from the outside like an infringement of human liberty – hence the hostility to belief in an objective God evinced by that stream of modern thought which goes back to Hegel and Fichte[3] – is discovered, within the world of religious experience (unless that experience itself gets perverted), to constitute the necessary condition of genuine freedom. That is to say, the utterly gracious presence and act of God in the believer liberate him from the bondage of a self-centred will and enable him to will and to do the good.

As pointed out above, this is an essentially relational concept of the religious life. It is perfectly true that the human will provides the analogical base for our understanding of the divine will in what has indeed been called a 'voluntarist' theistic metaphysic;[4] but it is the *relation* between the divine will and the human will that forms the heart of the Christian religion in its understanding of the divine creative purpose and of the salvific gracious acts of God in incarnation and inspiration. It is God's will that prescribes the religious way and it is God's will that enables and actualises man's response, not by coercion overriding the human will, but by grace, which both respects and enhances human freedom. This paradox of grace – a unique but essentially relational phenomenon – lies at the heart of Christian experience and understanding and it is astonishing to come across a Christian theologian who has so totally lost his grasp of it as to prefer the purely self-assertive voluntarism of Schopenhauer and Nietzsche as a basis for reformulating the essence of Christianity.

Cupitt's espousal of voluntarism is even more extreme than this brief discussion might suggest. It is not only the religious life and the religious ideal that are held to be a product of the human will. Man's whole world, not just his religious world, is said to be a purely human construction. What the Christian tradition ascribes to the creative will of God is here transferred entirely to the creative will of man. Instead of being derivatively free and dependent, receptive and responsive in his subsidiary creativity, man is, in an unqualified sense, the maker of all things and the maker of all value. It is for this reason that Cupitt is rightly accused of Prometheanism.

Another, less extravagant characteristic of this conception of religion is its *pragmatism*. Eschewing theory, it concentrates the religious mind on practice, on Christianity as a *way*, a set of policies and attitudes and ideals, inspiring Christian commitment and Christian action. When Cupitt speaks of seeking to develop a consistently ethical view of God, it is clear that he thinks it necessary to translate all 'God-talk' into talk of a guiding ethical and spiritual *ideal*. Not surprisingly, the figure of Kant is invoked as that of the philosopher who most singlemindedly brought out the primacy of the ethical and the purely ethical significance of religion, including Church doctrine and Church ritual. The significance of Kant will be assessed in chapter five; but it is already clear that Cupitt is going further than Kant in proposing a complete translation of all God-talk into practical terms.

Against this trend, it has to be argued that, while Christianity is indeed a practical faith, its ethical core depends on and flows from its recognition of transcendent goodness and its commerce with the ethical and spiritual resources of transcendent goodness. Once again, Christian ethical practice is a relational phenomenon, love of the neighbour being inspired by and enabled by the love of God for all his creatures. Certainly we need to develop a consistently ethical view of God. But that does not mean the substitution of an ethical ideal for the idea of God and the translation of God-talk into the language of pragmatism. A consistently ethical view of God is a view which sees in the infinite source and goal of all there is an absolute objective moral standard, a holy will, and a perfect love that constitute the pattern for our practical endeavours and the inspiration of our ethical commitments.

Where an ethical ideal is held to be a purely human (albeit collective) product or creation, it is bound to possess a certain arbitrariness. However noble, it can only be offered and commended as one possibility among others, something which, one hopes, men and women will find attractive and inspiring and worth the commitment and discipline of a moral and religious life. But where an ethical ideal is held to reflect the ultimate nature and purpose of things, its appeal ceases to be arbitrary or optional. It is seen to be objective and compelling – compelling not in a way that overrides freedom and responsibility but morally compelling as the ideal behind the whole creation and the law of our life whereby alone we find our own true good. This objective good, this perfect love is also, as I have been insisting at each point against Cupitt's view, the very basis and resource for the overcoming of our inability to love and to act well out of our own resources.

Finally, the understanding of religion which we are considering here is characterised as *internalised* or *interiorised*. Religion is explicitly denied to be a relational affair – a way of life evoked and sustained by a power *not* ourselves. My reaction to this has already been given in the paragraphs about the *subjectivism* of this view. The fact that the Spirit of the living God is most intimately encountered *within*, in the cave of the heart, must not be misconstrued as meaning that life in the Spirit is no more than a set of inner states and disciplines, cultivated and affirmed against a materialist or hedonist philosophy of life. Certainly the Christian religion is much concerned with purity of heart. A purely external religion has been rejected and condemned from New Testament times on. But Christian purity of heart is not an achievement. It is a gift. It is a quality of the interior life which results from experience of grace, forgiveness and divine indwelling. Such an interiorised religion loses its essence and its power where God is no longer thought of as its real and objective source and ground.

In the second half of this chapter, I turn to consider Cupitt's treatment of some of the key figures whom he selects to indicate what he takes to be the only possible stance for Christians to adopt in face of the pressures of modernity – namely, this interiorised, pragmatic, voluntarist and expressive understanding of religion. The figures in question are Pascal, Jung, Schweitzer, Kierkegaard and Wittgenstein.

It should be said at once that this list is a highly selective one. In no way are these figures as determinative of twentieth-century Christianity as Galileo, Darwin, Freud, Marx and Nietzsche are of twentieth-century civilisation in general. Moreover, each of these purported modern Church fathers is an extremely ambiguous figure, susceptible of very different interpretations. In each case, only one side of their complex personalities and thought might be supposed to lead in the extreme direction taken by Cupitt.

Blaise Pascal, the seventeenth-century French mathematician and religious philosopher, represents an early and somewhat implausible reaction to the threat posed by the rise of modern science and its apparent universal mechanism. His total separation of the spheres of science and faith, his rejection of any metaphysical concern on the part of the religious mind, his location of the sphere of faith solely within, in the believer's heart, these motifs do *not* constitute a tenable position for anyone today who is seriously concerned with the impact of modernity on Christianity. It was, of course, a religiously powerful response in its time, just because of the importance of inwardness in religion, which I have already acknowledged to be a dominant factor in religious epistemology since St Augustine. Pascal succeeds very well in bringing out the intense subjectivity and passion of religious faith. But it is quite clear that Pascal himself was convinced that it was with God that he had to do in such experience, just as he was convinced that in responding to Christ he was responding to the God who addressed him in Christ. Such a total concern with inwardness, however, has been proved unwise and vulnerable. Cupitt shows how easily such a repudiation of theoretical objectivity and metaphysics can lead to concentration on inner states themselves rather than on what those states are believed to mediate, namely, experiential knowledge of God. The danger of exclusive stress on the human mediation of knowledge of God through the heart (and through Christ) is that the reference beyond to the one encountered by these means gets lost. But that Pascal himself meant such a reference beyond is quite clear. Even his token gesture in the direction of theoretical objectivity – his notorious 'wager' argument for acting on the supposition that

God is real – shows that he, Pascal, was least of all concerned to resort to a subjectivist or expressivist understanding of faith, in the senses discussed above.

It is doubly mistaken, therefore, to endorse Pascal's separation of religious inwardness from theoretical objectivity and then to read the former purely subjectively. It is even more mistaken to generalise from this early and untenable reaction to modernity and say that 'either you can claim to have an objective God, like Descartes, or you can have an authentic Christian faith, like Pascal'.[5] Without wishing to support Karl Barth's position on the epistemology of Christian knowledge of God, the name of that leading twentieth-century theologian is a standing refutation of the view that 'the claims of theological realism and of religious seriousness now pull in opposite directions'.[6] The case of Barth (and its own vulnerabilities) will be considered in the next chapter, where I shall also show, in more general terms, how theological realism is of the essence of religious seriousness, not least in relation to a modern scientific understanding of the world. But the supposition that concern with an objective God lacks religious seriousness must be shown up at once as lacking all plausibility. Moreover, Pascal himself clearly was concerned with an objective God, even if he thought (mistakenly) that metaphysics was entirely the wrong way of approaching the matter. To put the point in more recent terms, the fact that what John Henry Newman called 'notional assent' requires to be turned into 'real assent',[7] by dint of religious experience and the conviction of the heart, does not mean that the latter is any less objective than the former. Newman was in fact much more plausible than Pascal in retaining a place for notional assent and for appropriate modes of argument to support belief in God, while at the same time stressing the role of conscience and firsthand experience, if that belief is to come alive.

Carl Gustav Jung, the former associate of Freud and

founder of analytical psychology, is a most unlikely figure to be elevated to the status of a modern Church father. His positive appraisal of the function of religion in psychic health and well-being is undoubtedly of great interest and can be used in religious psychology within the context of Christian belief. But Jung himself deliberately cultivated the kind of ambiguity which we discerned in Pascal, although against the latter's intentions. Jung concentrated on the human pheno-menon of religion as a factor in psychic health and refused to commit himself one way or another on the question of the 'reality' of God in anything other than a purely psychological sense. However, Jung's deliberate agnosticism on this central issue should prevent us from labelling him a 'non-realist' in his philosophy of religion. In fact he had no philosophy of religion. It is always possible to interpret him either way. The Christian realist will interpret Jung's account of the human idea of God and its function in life as reflecting the meta-physical reality of God as appropriated by the human mind. The unbeliever will interpret him in purely humanistic terms. What one cannot do is to claim Jung's own authority for the latter view. And even if one could, the relevance of what would then be Jung's atheistic, albeit positive, treatment of the phenomenon of religion for the Church's understanding of its faith would be quite minimal. As with all other forms of atheism, it would require rebuttal, not endorsement, by the Christian apologist.

The case of Jung, it may be observed at this point, illu-strates the problem which the Christian apologist has with all theories of the alleged object of religious belief as a purely human projection. As John Bowker shows in *The Sense of God*,[8] projectionist theories, whether hostile or sympathetic, are quite unable to disprove the possibility that humanly constructed ideas of God are in fact more or less appropriate human responses to the reality of God evoking them.

Albert Schweitzer, the German organist and biblical scholar

who abandoned the academic life for that of medical mission, plays a dual role in Cupitt's strategy. He is alleged to ex-emplify what happens when a thoroughly modern and critical view is taken of the Christian Scriptures, and he is also alleged to exemplify the purely voluntarist, ethical stance which is bound to replace authoritarian, dogmatic religion. For all the criticisms that have been levelled against his own authoritarian, paternalist and old-fashioned style, Schweitzer's ethical commitment and practice as a doctor in Africa remain extremely impressive. But his peculiar, critical interpretation of the New Testament has long been superseded by much more careful and balanced, critical treatments of the Gospels. Schweitzer's *Quest of the Historical Jesus*[9] can in no way be thought of as the last word in Gospel criticism. No serious New Testament scholar now holds, as Schweitzer did, that Jesus went to his death, intending thereby to force the hand of God to bring about the end-time. And in any case Schweitzer himself did not react to his own alleged critical discoveries by abandoning a realist faith in God, despite the disparity between his reconstruction of Jesus's motives and his own understanding of a compelling ethical vocation. To speak of Schweitzer as purely voluntarist in religion is again to interpret an ambiguous figure very one-sidedly in the interests of a theory already adopted. In fact Schweitzer is much less ambiguous than Jung in respect of belief in God. He may have been unduly wilful in his manner of working at Lambarene, and he may have failed to appreciate the priority of grace in a Christian understanding of God's action in and through the believer and the Church. But a perusal of his lectures in Birmingham in 1922 on *Christianity and the Religions of the World*[10] shows quite clearly that Schweitzer saw it as of the essence of Christianity to have taught and inspired an 'ethic of men who together strive to attain to a perfect yielding of themselves to the will of God'. We are to become 'forces of God's ethical personality'. Indeed it is the conception of

God as 'an ethical Personality' that is the special contribution of the Judaeo-Christian religion to mankind. So, however radical a reconstruction of the life and death of Jesus is to be found in Schweitzer's New Testament interpretation, he still saw the transcendent claims of God's ethical will as having inspired that life and death as it has done the lives of Christians ever since. There is even less reason for us to follow Cupitt in interpreting Schweitzer as a non-realist in religion than there is for us to follow Schweitzer in his so-called 'consistent eschatology'.

Søren Kierkegaard, the Danish philosopher and precursor of Christian existentialism, is a much more plausible candidate for a modern father of the Church than either Jung or Schweitzer, more plausible even than Pascal. For Kierkegaard combines Pascal's intense subjectivity and passion with a developed theory of religious subjectivity as the only appropriate road to faith and to knowledge of God. He concedes less to the scope of science and he shows more clearly the necessity of an existential leap of faith. Certainly he rejected with passion any metaphysical attempt to secure the objectivity of God. He was the father of all existentialist hostility to objectivisation in any form. The individual's inwardness and subjectivity, affirming itself against the crowd, against scientific rationality, against conformity in state or Church, are the only point at which God may be known, experienced and obeyed.

It is not surprising that Cupitt should claim Kierkegaard's support for his own, anti-metaphysical, interiorised understanding of religion. Kierkegaard's ambiguity opens up this path of interpretation as readily as any of the figures whom we are considering in this chapter. Yet despite the stress on subjectivity, a purely subjectivist interpretation is least plausible of all in the case of Kierkegaard. Justice must be done to the fact that, in Professor Stewart Sutherland's words 'Kierkegaard's thought and writing is dominated, one might even say "domineered" throughout by the conception of a transcendent and sovereign God'.[11] Admittedly, for Keirkegaard, such a God can only be known 'indirectly' in and through the inwardness of faith. But even there faith's object is God as he reveals himself, pardoxically, in the utter contingency of a historical incarnation, pictured inforgettably in Kierkegaard's parable of the king who becomes a peasant in order to woo the humble maiden. Kierkegaard's hostility to any rational attempt at justification of this understanding of faith is extreme; but that his is a *relational* view of faith, in a way quite unlike Cupitt's own view, is undeniable.

But, even when interpreted in a more balanced way, Kierkegaard could never become more than a goad and a challenge to the faith and practice of a Christianity already understood as man's response to God's holy will and revelation. A balanced interpretation of Kierkegaard still portrays an unbalanced thinker. For all the dangers of a state religion, a merely public faith and a philosophically neutral concept of God, there is no need to be so paradoxical, so individualistic and so hostile to natural theology as Kierkegaard was in his polemical writings. As I argue throughout this book, a deeply felt and authentic Christian faith not only can but must include the readiness to think through and share its relation to all elements of human knowledge, to science, history and philosophy. The very possibility of Cupitt's misappropriation of Kierkegaard reveals the insecurity of the latter's stance as a spokesman for the truth of Christianity. Truth, subjectively encountered, cannot be set against objective truth.

The philosopher, Ludwig Wittgenstein's appearance at the end of Cupitt's series of television programmes on *The Sea of Faith* must have struck the vast majority of viewers as quite beyond the bounds of intelligibility. Wittgenstein is a fascinating figure and a major influence in twentieth-century philosophy, though even in philosophy his views are highly controversial and subject to diverse interpretations. His scattered remarks on religion and a number of anecdotes by friends have given philosophers of religion much to ponder, but, with so little to go on, it is hardly surprising that even greater disagreement is to be found over Wittgenstein on religion than over Wittgenstein on philosophy.[12] The idea that Wittgenstein could ever become a major source of the Church's own self-understanding in the twentieth century is quite bizarre. No one less like a modern Church father could possibly be imagined.

Given the obscurity of the subject, I make no claim to authority for the following remarks, but I think they give a more accurate picture than what we find in Cupitt's presentation.

In philosophy, Wittgenstein is often supposed to have moved from a realist, yet virtually positivist position in the *Tractatus Logico-Philosophicus*[13] of 1921 to a more Kantian, constructivist philosophy of language in the posthumously published *Philosophical Investigations*.[14] ('Positivism' is the name given to the view that factual knowledge depends entirely on what is presented to the senses. 'Constructivism' is the name given to the view that the human mind, through the imposition or projection of its own concepts on experience, 'constructs' its own world.) It seems however that both the earlier and the later philosophies of Wittgenstein have been seriously misunderstood. In the *Tractatus*, far from setting forth a form of 'logical positivism', restricting meaning to logico/mathematical truth and to statements corresponding to empirically verifiable states of affairs, Wittgenstein was chiefly concerned to indicate the limits of factual discourse, beyond which the much more important ethical and 'mystical' truths could only be *shown*, not stated. What Wittgenstein abandoned in his later philosophy was not this fundamental position but only the particular theory of correspondence between propositions and states of affairs in the world. This does not necessarily mean that he adopted a constructivist philosophy whereby human beings constitute, by their own concepts, the world in which they live. Certainly, for the later Wittgenstein, there is more of a conflation of the 'sayable' and the 'showable'. But what matters is not so much what we create linguistically as what we are constrained to say. In all its manifold uses, human language shows rather than states the basic shape of the world in which we live. The basic facts of the empirical world – the reality, for instance, of the external world and of other minds – are shown by our forms of speech in a way that makes scepticism on these matters quite impossible. Similarly, ethical and spiritual values are *shown* in our moral and religious forms of life. So even in Wittgenstein's case, I do not think that a purely interiorised, projectionist interpretation of religion holds. These are, as I say, very controversial matters, but I notice that a number of Wittgenstein's followers have used his methods of analysis in the interests of a much more realist understanding of theistic belief than Wittgenstein himself, still less Cupitt, would allow.[15]

But in any case the Church theologian is unlikely to agree that divine truth is as unsayable as even the later Wittgenstein thought. The force of Wittgenstein's stress on what must be shown in life is very great, but there is no reason to think that we are driven back to such a parsimonious conception of the sayable as to rule out careful use of extended analogical and metaphorical uses of language in the expression of truth about God and his revelation. (Even the 'apophatic' tradition in Christian theology, which stresses the transcendent mystery of God about which we can only keep silent, requires an express tradition of belief on which to operate.)

Of the five figures considered in this section, all are highly ambiguous and unrepresentative. Two, Jung and Wittgenstein, are as ambiguous in their own fields, psychology and philosophy, as they are in relation to religion.

A third, Schweitzer, is highly idiosyncratic, both in his biblical interpretation and in his practical discipleship, impressive though the latter is. Only Pascal and Kierkegaard could reasonably be said to have grasped an essential aspect of the religious response to modernity – namely, the passionate inwardness that must indeed resist all forms of mechanistic, depersonalising philosophy. But at the same time both Pascal and Kierkegaard failed to integrate their understanding of the inwardness of faith with other knowledge, and indeed with what faith implies about God, the universe and man. None of Cupitt's modern Church fathers, therefore, can carry the weight that he places on their shoulders. We can only conclude that Cupitt's prior commitment to an anti-metaphysical, expressivist, interiorised and pragmatic understanding of religious faith has dictated his choice of five figures on the margins of modern Christianity who *can*, with varying degrees of implausibility, be interpreted as pointing in this direction.

4

Theism in the modern world

My double aim of showing both the idiosyncrasy and the falsehood of a purely expressivist view of Christianity will now be advanced by a survey of alternative options. I shall sketch in this chapter a number of current movements and thinkers in modern Christian theology and philosophy of religion in order to provide a more balanced idea of the possibility of theism in the age of science.

We may begin with the names of the two German-speaking Protestant theologians who dominated mid twentieth-century Christian theology, Rudolf Bultmann and Karl Barth. We may not find ourselves in complete agreement with either of these writers, but they are both worth taking very seriously indeed, not only because of their enormous range and inherent stature as Christian thinkers, but also because each, in his different way, was conscious of the problem set for Christian faith by post-Enlightenment modernity, including the historical critical method in its application to the Bible. But they were both also highly conscious of the claims of God and his Word. Their interest and importance lie in the ways in which they tried to bring a powerful theology of the Word to bear upon modern man and modern culture.

Rudolf Bultmann has been criticised, no doubt rightly, for an excessive reliance on existentialist philosophy, an uncritical acceptance of a closed mechanistic view of physical science, and an excessively radical use of critical method in the interest of 'demythologising' the Christian gospel as found in the New Testament writings. Yet the overall purpose of Bultmann's theology and in part his achievement were thoroughly positive: an unqualified acceptance of modern science, a recognition of authentic human life and responsibility as transcending the limits of science, and a conviction of the power of the Christian Gospel to overcome the evil in man and to sustain man's authenticity under God's Word.[1] Bultmann sought to let the Word of God be heard, untrammelled by outmoded, pre-scientific categories of thought. He was just as convinced as Cupitt of the capacity, indeed the necessity, of biblical criticism, to enable the modern reader to get behind the husk of first-century cosmology which had of course coloured the biblical writers' imagination. But unlike Cupitt, Bultmann does not see the kernel of Christian faith as lying simply in its ethical and spiritual ideal. He is much too aware of the claim from beyond and the resources from beyond, which constitute the heart of Christianity, to let go of these key elements in the tradition. Even if we think his critical methods extreme, his philosophical presuppositions somewhat one-sided, and his understanding of science defective, we can still salute in Bultmann a thoroughly modern mind, at the same time aware of and loyal to divine transcendence. Perhaps most to be regretted is his unwillingness to support this latter conviction by argument or to hold the scientific, the existential and the metaphysical together in the interests of doing justice both to modernity and to the Gospel. Later in this chapter we shall encounter more satisfactory attempts at such an integration.

Opposition to natural theology of an even more extreme kind is, regretfully, a salient characteristic of Karl Barth's theology. Moreover, Barth showed a certain cavalier indifference to the result of biblical criticism. But the greatness of Barth as a truly modern Christian theologian lay in his thorough understanding of post-Enlightenment thought and his detailed working out of the consequence of an entirely revelation-based Christian theology.[2] Barth's theological epistemology, moreover, is developed precisely in reaction to the perceived limitations of post-Enlightenment modernity. To deny either the intellectual power or the religious seriousness of Barth's theological realism can only be described as absurd. And even when one questions his rejection of natural theology, his failure to listen to the biblical scholars and his extremely negative assessment of other religions, one still learns a great deal from his explication of Christian doctrine, organised as it is around his central recognition of Jesus Christ as God's reconciling Word to man.

The debate between Barth and Bultmann – the former accusing the latter of capitulating too readily to post-Enlightenment philosophy, the latter accusing the former of failing to appreciate the extent of the reinterpretations required if the Gospel is to be preached to modern man – is still the best place at which to introduce the enquirer to the possibilities of theistic faith in the context of twentieth-century western culture. But of course the debate has gone on, with further refinements, among their respective pupils, who themselves have now nearly completed their own life's work. Among Bultmann's pupils we may mention Gunther Bornkamm, Ernst Käsemann and Gerhard Ebeling, all of whom illustrate the religious power of German Lutheranism in its engagement with modern culture. We note, in the work of these men, a certain tendency to moderate the more extreme elements in Bultmann's work – a less negative use of biblical criticism, a more optimistic assessment of our ability to reconstruct the life and teaching of the historical Jesus, a greater recognition of the worth of traditional Christian doctrine, even under existentialist interpretation.[3] Among Barth's pupils we may mention Thomas F. Torrance, who has expounded theological realism with great power, precisely in relation to a post-Einsteinian understanding of the physical universe. This correlation of fundamental science and fundamental theology is very striking and puts a definite question mark against the naive assumption that modern science makes belief in God impossible.[4] Another Barthian, Helmut Gollwitzer, provided a powerful theological (though not philosophical) defence of the existence of God in the earlier context of the short-lived, 'death of God' debate in the 1960s.[5]

Continental suspicion of natural theology has still marred the contributions even of Bultmann's and Barth's pupils to the presentation and defence of Christian theism. One of the most notable features of the next generation of German theologians is the recognition of the need to combine theology and philosophy in the refutation of atheism. This is most evident in the work of Wolfhart Pannenberg, whose book, *Theology and the Philosophy of Science*,[6] may be set in stark contrast to the books of Cupitt as a prime example of an alternative possibility for Christian theology in the age of science. Pannenberg's willingness to undergird a novel interpretation of theistic ontology (theory of being) with philosophical arguments is most impressive. Even if one disagrees with Pannenberg's ontology, his work exemplifies the serious possibilities that exist of a philosophically and theologically informed rational defence of Christian theism today.

Jürgen Moltmann's work, especially his recent books, *The Trinity and the Kingdom of God*,[7] and *God in Creation*,[8] is less philosophically acute, but a standing refutation of the charge that incarnational and trinitarian theology is necessarily conservative and oppressive in character. On the contrary, we might wish to question the extent of Moltmann's radicalism. But the power of his theological commitment, precisely on the basis of christological and trinitarian understanding, to the political liberation of mankind, is very great. Just as Pannenberg's work illustrates the possibility of serious theistic belief in the light of modern science, so Moltmann's work illustrates the possibility of serious theistic belief not only in the light of, but contributing to, contemporary political and social radicalism.

Eberhard Jüngel's contribution is less accessible than that of Pannenberg or Moltmann, but his *God as the Mystery of the World*,[9] deserves particular mention for its resolute attempt to show how God may be spoken of in an increasingly secularised world. Jüngel's sensitivity to the cognitive power of metaphorical and analogical uses of language (that is to say, their ability to yield some *knowledge* of God), together with his theological seriousness in articulating a Christian anthropology in the light of God's making himself available to man, represents a salutory antidote to the literal-minded conviction that all non-empirical language can only be expressive of ideals.

These chiefly German Protestant theologians can be seen to have demonstrated two basic facts which belie Cupitt's assertion that there is no alternative to a purely expressivist, voluntarist form of Christian faith today. One is an anthropological, the other a theological fact. The anthropological fact is the implausibility of a reductionist, physicalist conception of man. Man's freedom, his openness to the future, his quest for authenticity, all transcend the ability of modern science to explain. Thus they invite religious explanation. The theological fact is the existential power of a critically appropriated understanding of the Word of God in the Christian Scriptures and tradition. It is my contention that only theological realism – realism about God the Creator and God the Redeemer – can do justice to these facts.

Interest in the possibility of theological realism in the modern world now leads us to consider the work of some leading Roman Catholic theologians in the twentieth century. Rather belatedly, especially where acceptance of historical critical methods of biblical study and interpretation is concerned, but with remarkable enthusiasm and success since the Second Vatican Council, Roman Catholic theology has sought to come to grips with modern science, historiography and philosophy and to restate Christian faith in God and in Christ precisely in the face of modern questions. Just because Roman Catholic theological self-understanding is so powerfully reinforced by the institution of the Church, there has been less temptation – though there has been some – to capitulate to modernity uncritically.

An exception to the adverb 'belatedly' which I used just now was the work of Pierre Teilhard de Chardin, which antedates the Second Vatican Council but which was somewhat frowned on by the official Church. Nevertheless his attempt to combine Christian theology and spirituality with a thorough grasp of cosmic and biological evolutionary theory illustrates very well the kind of synthesis that, for all its faults, is possible for a thoroughly modern Christian mind. The point I wish to single out for comment from *The Phenomenon of Man*[10] is this: Teilhard shows how the very fact of matter's capacity to organise itself in such a way as to evolve mind requires us to posit mind behind the whole process. He shows the greater reasonableness of interpreting the universe from the standpoint of its highest product, viz, the 'noosphere', the world of mind, than that of reducing the more complicated to the less complicated and trying to interpret mind in terms of the combination of material particles alone. This is an example of the kind of consideration which I shall explore in greater detail in chapter six, and which positively requires us to question the viability of reductionist science. Moreover it does so on the basis of scientific discovery, not just on the basis of an inherited theological scheme. It is precisely this kind of consideration which a realist, theistic metaphysic can make sense of, but which an expressivist view totally ignores.

Turning to more recent Roman Catholic thinkers, I will mention three, Bernard Lonergan, Karl Rahner, and Hans Küng. Each in his own way has made a remarkable effort to think through the doctrines of the Christian faith in the course of a relentless engagement with modernity rather than a subjectivist capitulation to modernity that leaves its difficulties unexplored.

Bernard Lonergan, especially in his books *Insight*[11] and *Method in Theology*,[12] has made a major contribution towards clarifying both the situation in which the modern theologian must do his work and the intellectual operations which must be performed if that work is to be done responsibly today. The modern theologian must indeed appropriate the critical and historical consciousness which differentiates our age from the classical ages of faith. But he must also integrate the workings of common sense, science, scholarship, philosophy and religion, if he is to avoid partial and one-sided approaches to reality such as those of the empiricists and the idealists. Lonergan describes the increasingly comprehensive enlargements of a man's horizon that occur as he acquires a critical awareness of scientific, moral and religious realities. Lonergan's writings are an excellent antidote to that state – which has afflicted many philosophers since the time of Kant – of being bemused by the idea that the human subject is cut off from the real world by its own categories and concepts. For he shows clearly how the operations of the human mind, far from obscuring reality, let alone constituting reality, enable us to obtain a differentiated awareness of physical, moral, metaphysical and divine reality – the latter, of course, in so far as God gives himself to be known by the human mind.

Karl Rahner might be thought to be somewhat too Kantian in his method of defending the possibility of religious and theological awareness in the modern world. Accepting Kant's method of concentration on the human subject as itself prescribing or imposing the basic conditions of all human knowledge, Rahner tries to spell out the ultimate presuppositions of our experience of subjectivity and personhood. He draws attention to man's self-transcendence and openness to the world and to his fellow men. Such openness cannot be accounted for in naturalistic terms. In it are disclosed the infinite transcendence and absolute mystery of being that constitute the ultimate background or horizon to our experience of personal and interpersonal existence. This analysis of infinite transcendence as the condition of human self-transcendence provides Rahner with a philosophical point of connection for explaining the reference of Christian talk of God.[13] In the sequel, I shall try to indicate, in a less indirect and roundabout way, the features in man's experience of being a person that modern science indeed fails to account for and which might well be thought indicative of the reality of God.

No one has succeeded better at a popular level in the task of Christian apologetics for today than the dissident Roman Catholic theologian, Hans Küng, in his two big books, *On Being a Christian*[14] and *Does God Exist?*.[15] Particularly in the latter, Küng faces the challenge of modern atheism in its various forms with great sensitivity. While seeing the point of the criticisms of religion and belief in God that are associated with the names of Feuerbach, Marx, Freud and Nietzsche, he turns the tables on each, pressing the question of the adequacy of their arguments and the ability of their world views to account for all the features of experience. Of special interest is the way in which Küng brings out the implications of man's fundamental trust in reality, notwithstanding the evidently alienating effect of modern naturalism. Coupled with his exposition, in the earlier book, of a positive and radical Christian faith in God for today, Küng's apologetic goes a long way towards refuting the idea that theism is bound to disappear in the context of modernity.

Unlike the majority of the German Protestant theologians considered in the previous section, these Roman Catholic thinkers are not afraid to give Christian theism a genuinely philosophical underpinning. They are perhaps most successful in showing the weakness of the arguments for atheism and the inability of scientific naturalism to account for, or do justice to, the phenomenon of man. We shall take up these points in our own attempt to state the case for theism, hopefully without quite such cumbersome philosophical apparatus.

In this brief survey of alternative options to an expressivist interpretation of religion, we turn next to a school of theology, most prominent in America, known as process theology, so called because of its preference for a dynamic analysis of reality in terms of 'becoming' rather than a static analysis in terms of 'being'. In some ways this school might be thought to be at a disadvantage in the philosophical climate of modernity in that it is entirely based on a particular metaphysical system, namely that of Alfred North Whitehead. Indeed, as a flourishing metaphysical school, process thought is very much an exception in the context of the mainly anti-metaphysical, analytical, tradition of philosophy that has grown out of British empiricism. Yet Whitehead's philosophy is undoubtedly a modern, science-based metaphysic, attempting to unify all our knowledge, external and internal, doing justice as much to felt experience and human creativity as to observation of nature and its constituents. In this, it faces up to the weaknesses of positivist and reductionist science very well. It shows their inadequacy to account for the whole of our experience of the world, including ourselves, and at the same time advances a powerful alternative metaphysic, unifying the physical and the mental throughout the continuum from matter or energy up to consciousness and reason. Reality as such must be thought of in such a way as to do justice to emergent properties right up the evolutionary scale. Novelty in nature and creativity in man exemplify the same basic characteristics of all the self-transcending processes that we experience. This metaphysic develops into a natural theology. For Whitehead's philosophy requires God as the self-actualising principle of creativity behind the whole emergent process.

Whitehead's philosophy has been taken up by a number of

theologians, notably Charles Hartshorne, whose followers include John Cobb, Norman Pittenger, David Griffin and, in an interesting combination of existentialism and process thought, Schubert Ogden. We cannot explore the writings of these authors here; nor need we discuss the difficulties which other philosophical theologians have had with their willingness to subsume the concept of God under the general categories of process metaphysics. Our interest lies simply in the natural theology of these writers, the way in which they share the Whiteheadian perception of the necessity of postulating the reality of God, if we are to do justice both to scientific knowledge and to experience of personhood and rationality. Thus John Cobb, in his *A Christian Natural Theology*[16] follows Whitehead in developing a non-dualist picture of nature and man suggestive of a divine principle of order behind the manifest order of the cosmic process. And Schubert Ogden, in his *The Reality of God*,[17] shows the necessity of postulating an ultimate ground of confidence in the significance and worth of our life in the world.

By contrast with these all-embracing metaphysical theories, which offer an ultimate *explanation* of the world, including natural science and human subjectivity, Cupitt's bare assertion of ethical and spiritual value against a meaningless natural world strikes the enquiring mind as arbitrary and deeply incoherent.

Much careful, if less exciting work has been done by a number of recent and contemporary British theologians in rethinking and re-presenting the essential heart of Christian doctrine in the light of modern science and historiography. I will restrict myself to the Anglican contribution, ranging my six examples in a spectrum from conservative to liberal. It is important to realise that liberal as well as conservative theologians appreciate the case for theism in the modern world. Moreover, like the process theologians, they are not afraid, on religious grounds, of natural theology, as most continental Protestants are.

Eric Mascall's numerous writings constitute a fresh and spirited defence of a broadly traditional 'Thomist' Christian theology. ('Thomism' is the name given to the kind of theology which stems from the teaching of the medieval saint and doctor of the Church, Thomas Aquinas.) Excessively conservative in biblical theology – the force and scope of biblical criticism seeming to escape him – Mascall comes into his own in natural and doctrinal theology, enabling the Anglican reader to see the rationality and point of classical Christian theism. Two of his books may be mentioned here, *He Who Is*,[18] and the Bampton Lectures, *Christian Theology and Natural Science*.[19] *He Who Is* not only expounds the traditional arguments for the existence of God; it also contains a defence – against the dominant post-Enlightenment philosophy in the English-speaking world, empiricism – of our ability to grasp the nature of finite things in their dependence on the infinite. A more detailed engagement with the world of modern science is to be found in the Bampton Lectures, where Mascall explores cosmology and creation, free-will and determinism, mind and brain, and the origin and evolution of life, in an attempt to show both the compatibility of religion and science, and also the incompleteness and insufficiency of a purely scientific view of the world.

Austin Farrer, schooled in the same Thomist tradition as Mascall, reveals a greater originality and power of argument in his writings, ranging from *Finite and Infinite*[20] to *Faith and Speculation*.[21] Farrer was first and foremost a philosophical theologian. His articulation and defence of a theistic view of the world and, especially in the later books, of an understanding of providence and divine action (and correlatively of why God permits suffering and evil in his world) are very impressive. And his little book, *A Science of God?*,[22] remains a model of how to think through the relation between a scientific and a theistic view of the world. At each stage, we find Farrer arguing against the empiricists and the positivists, holding together the whole range of factors, rational, historical and experiential, that suggest the theistic view. But he was also most adept at sketching, in his more occasional works, what I call the inner rationality of Christian doctrine. The facility with which he anticipates and meets objections and the clarity with which he shows what can be said, precisely in the context of modern knowledge, about belief in God and the implications of that belief, make Austin Farrer's philosophical theology, perhaps of all those mentioned in this chapter, the most telling and persuasive alternative to Cupitt's position.

Better known than Farrer, though curiously isolated in the philosophical and theological worlds, is the figure of John Macquarrie. His *Principles of Christian Theology*[23] is one of the few attempts at a systematic theology from the pen of a contemporary Anglican. Moreover, its first main section, entitled 'Philosophical Theology', sets out to provide a 'new style natural theology'. Part of the groundwork for this was already prepared in the book's Introduction where the spheres of science and theology are carefully demarcated. But the starting point of natural theology for Macquarrie is an existential analysis of man, an anthropology sensitive both to man's alienation and to his capacity for faith. Religious faith takes its rise from a revelatory experience of 'holy being', which Macquarrie equates with the God of religion. For Macquarrie does not rest content with existential analysis. He links it with an ontology of 'being', the mysterious transcendent source of all beings, that both lets them be and manifests itself as 'holy being' in and through the beings of the world, especially human beings. This approach continues to characterise Macquarrie's more recent work, the books, *In Search of Humanity*[24] and *In Search of Deity*.[25] The former develops an anthropology of human self-transcendence that points, not least in art and religion, to the reality of God as the source, support and goal of human life. The latter expounds what Macquarrie calls a 'dialectical' theism, explicitly advanced as a more persuasive alternative to classical theism than is reductionist atheism, typified by David Hume. For, as Macquarrie shows, nature itself, in man, transcends the physical by a creative advance into the spiritual. On the basis of this natural theology, Macquarrie has articulated a relatively conservative, broadly Catholic, systematic theology. There is thus a refreshing combination of novelty and tradition in his work.

In turning to the writings of the Bishop of Durham, David Jenkins, we move in the direction of the more liberal end of the spectrum – but not very far. For Jenkins's *Guide to the Debate about God*[26] and *Living with Questions*[27] show him to be a resolute defender of a properly understood theism, arguing for a 'post-Copernican natural theology' that matches human existence and the human situation with a God, the test of whose reality is practical. Jenkins faces up to the fact that the rise of modern science and technology has been accompanied, perhaps inevitably, by the rise of modern atheism. But that atheism, he argues, has been reinforced by the deadness of the modern Church. Only a practical witness to the living God can hope to reverse this trend, not least by helping to liberate man from the bondage of a science and technology run riot. Hence, in his *The Glory of Man*[28] and *The Contradiction of Christianity*,[29] he develops a Christian humanism and a political theology that find, precisely in the figure of Jesus Christ and in the incarnational and trinitarian theology to which reflection on his significance gives rise, the spiritual resources for a liberating confrontation with all forms of alienation and oppression. Practical witness to the love of God in setting people free is the strongest argument for the reality and effectiveness of that love.

The debate about God to which Jenkins wrote a guide in

1966 was of course the debate opened up by the astonishing success of Bishop John Robinson's book, *Honest to God*,[30] which eventually sold over one million copies. Looking back from the later vantage-point of engagement with Cupitt's work, we may well consider Robinson to be a relatively conservative figure. He was indeed no atheist, whatever ignorant critics may have said at the time. On the contrary, Robinson's work illustrates how a liberal or, as he preferred to be called, a radical theologian could maintain the heart of theism in the context of modernity, indicating precisely those aspects of experience which require us as modern men and women to become aware of the utterly personal source and goal of all there is. It is extremely instructive, then, to set Robinson's conviction that 'we are rooted and grounded wholly in Love' against Cupitt's purely naturalistic view of the context of human life. Admittedly, Robinson wrote loosely. His polemic against 'supranaturalism' was confusing and he exaggerated his own radicalism. But, as his later book *Exploration into God*[31] makes clear, he never abandoned his conviction that religion is a matter of response – response to ultimate reality experienced as personal. This awareness of being addressed, claimed and sustained from beyond as well as from within, differentiates Robinson's theology utterly from Cupitt's position now, as it did from Paul van Buren's at the time. The philosophy which undergirds Robinson's theology is the I-Thou philosophy of Martin Buber – an intuition of 'an ultimate relatedness in the very structure of our being'. He set such a view against both traditional supernatural theism *and* atheistic naturalism. Moreover his desire to go 'beyond the God of theism' reflected the entirely proper theological insistence on not treating God as *a* being among the beings, on a level, as it were, with worldly realities. He was quite prepared to speak of 'the transcendent source and goal of all being – in all things and through all things and above all things' as 'personal spirit'. For there are levels of reality, to which we have access in our experiences of value, which take us beyond the mathematical and quantitative regularities explored in science.

Finally, in this section, I shall mention Maurice Wiles, Regius Professor of Divinity in Oxford, whose writings exemplify, in a much clearer and more precise form, the liberal end of the spectrum. Wiles is notorious for his critical assault on a number of central Christian doctrines, notably the Incarnation and special providence. Elsewhere, I have taken issue with his scepticism on both these topics and questioned the adequacy of his attempts to 'remake' Christian doctrine.[32] Here I simply note his firm commitment to theism, notwithstanding his awareness of the significance of modern science and, especially, historical criticism. In his book, *Faith and the Mystery of God*,[33] Wiles endorses Schubert Ogden's conclusion 'that faith in God as the ground of confidence in life's ultimate meaning is the necessary condition of our existence as selves'. It is anthropological reflection on what it is to be a human being that prevents even liberal theologians such as Wiles from abandoning personal language in speaking of the ground of being. Indeed, Wiles goes on to develop an impressive case for belief in God as *spirit*.

I will bring this survey of theistic options in the context of modernity to a close by referring briefly to a number of Christian philosophers of religion (and of science) who are making significant contributions to the analysis and defence of theism today. Indeed the quality of such philosophical analysis may be deemed to be higher at present than for some decades.

From the United States comes a body of work by relatively conservative scholars of very high philosophical calibre. Alvin Plantinga, Nicholas Wolterstorff and George Mavrodes, in their different ways, have greatly enhanced our understanding of the rationality of religious belief. Their writings, however, exhibit an interesting and fruitful tension. On the one hand, Wolterstorff, and to a certain extent Plantinga are more concerned to demonstrate the inner rationality of a basic-faith stance than to try to justify that stance from an allegedly neutral point of view. Indeed they call upon recent philosophical attacks on 'foundationalism' (the theory that we have to build up all our human knowledge on incontrovertible foundations) to articulate the rationality of a view of the world which takes belief in God as basic. On this we may refer to Wolterstorff's *Reason within the Bounds of Religion*[34] and Plantinga's essays in *Rationality and Religious Belief*[35] and *Faith and Rationality*.[36] But, as Mavrodes points out in an article in this latter collection, Plantinga has also made significant contributions to the apologetic task of arguing for religious belief, both negatively in his writings on theodicy and positively in his remarkable defence of the ontological argument for the existence of God. Plantinga's views on these topics are most readily accessible in *God, Freedom and Evil*.[37] Mavrodes himself, in the article just mentioned and in *Belief in God*,[38] shows himself ready to give an affirmative answer both to the question 'Are we within our intellectual rights in believing in God?' and to the question 'Is there reason to suppose that belief in God is true?'. Whatever we may think of the foundationalist versus anti-foundationalist dispute, the sheer intellectual power of these writers' defence of the rationality of theism belies any easy assertion that belief in an objective God is impossible in the context of modernity.

A similar stress on the rationality of belief in God rather than on arguments for belief in God is to be found in the writings of John Hick, who has probably made the single most sustained contribution to the philosophy of religion in the last three decades. Of particular interest is the little book, *Why Believe in God?*,[39] which he wrote jointly with Michael Goulder. Hick's arguments rest almost entirely on the appeal to experience – an important, indeed essential, element in any case for theism, but somewhat vulnerable if taken by itself without supporting arguments.

Two philosophers of religion who have provided such supporting arguments are Basil Mitchell in *The Justification of Religious Belief,* [40] and Richard Swinburne in *The Existence of God.* [41] These books are particularly important for their use of probability theory in the construction of a cumulative case for belief in God, that is to say, the assemblage of a series of rational arguments that together support the hypothesis of there being an infinite creative mind behind the whole world process – a hypothesis, so these authors claim, finding confirmation in religious experience. Swinburne, in an earlier book, *The Coherence of Theism,* [42] defends the intelligibility of the view 'that there exists eternally an omnipresent spirit, free, creator of the universe, omnipotent, omniscient, perfectly good, and a source of moral obligation'. In this same group of philosophical apologetic writings may be included *Rational Theology and the Creativity of God* by Keith Ward, [43] a book which contains acute analysis of both the nature and the grounds of Christian theism.

Such work is often dismissed as abstract, dry and basically unreligious by critics aware of the spiritual depths of a genuinely religious faith in God. And many readers are persuaded of the greater 'religious' tone of the writings of expressivist and pragmatist philosophers of religion such as Cupitt. But this is a mistake. The philosophers of religion mentioned in the preceding paragraphs are selecting for analysis and defence elements explicit or implicit in the faith of the vast majority of ordinary believers. That is their function as philosophers of religion. A purely expressivist view, by contrast, however religiously deep it may sound at first hearing, has in fact emptied out the heart of Christian theism. Hence the necessity of singling out and subjecting to philosophical examination its irreducibly cognitive core.

I will add one more name to this list of authors whose work exemplifies alternative reactions to the challenge of modernity – that of Arthur Peacocke. His *Creation and the World of Science*[44] and *Intimations of Reality*[45] demonstrate not only the range and depth of current investigation of the relations between science and religion, but also a much more balanced assessment of the compatibility, indeed the interdependence, of the two than is to be found in the work of Cupitt. The possibility of a 'critical realism' in respect of theistic belief is evident in these writings as it is in all those mentioned in this chapter.

5

The significance of Kant

If two figures were to be singled out as lying behind the version of Christianity which Cupitt is proposing, they would be Kant and the Buddha. I shall have something to say about the latter in chapter eight. Here I concentrate attention on the figure of the great German Enlightenment philosopher, Immanuel Kant, whose thought has played so important a role in philosophy, including the philosophy of science, throughout the nineteenth and twentieth centuries, and whose critical philosophy has affected the whole way of looking at the world of many people hardly aware of his name. We all live in the 'post-Kantian' age.

The feature in Kant's philosophy which I want to stress as being so influential on the modern mind is his scepticism about the possibility of knowing reality as it is in itself. We may not immediately associate Kant with scepticism. Descartes's methodical scepticism is well known, as is its purpose – to re-establish firm knowledge on a secure foundation. Hume's 'mitigated' scepticism is also well known; though apart from the 'common things of life' it was a pretty thoroughgoing scepticism about the scope of human knowledge. And even where the common things of life are concerned, it is only habit or custom that, according to Hume, comes to our rescue and prevents an even more radical doubt. Kant, by contrast, provided a rigorous and fully worked out account of human knowledge, including all that Newtonian science had, as he thought, conclusively established. But Kant's was a sceptical view for all that, since by dint of his well-known 'Copernican revolution' he restricted factual knowledge to phenomena alone, to things, that is, as they *appear*, and professed complete scepticism about our theoretical ability to know things as they are in themselves.

Kant's Copernican revolution, like Copernicus' own, represented a marked shift of perspective, but in a diametrically opposite direction. Copernicus moved the focus of attention away from the earth, man's home, to the sun, thereby relativising our own human perspective. Kant focussed attention back on the human subject, identifying the salient characteristics of things as they appear to us in ordinary experience and in Newtonian science, as stemming not from the nature of things as they are in themselves, but from modes of apprehension peculiar to us. Things appear as they do to us, not because that is how they are irrespective of human observers, but rather because that is how our minds process the data received by the senses. Our very basic categories such as substance and causation, in terms of which we identify things and persons and the way they interact, are a priori concepts of the understanding which we bring to experience rather than find there. And even more remarkably, for Kant the basic notions of time and space, in terms of which all experience is temporally structured and the whole world spatially extended, are also imposed by our own modes of apprehension. Things appear to us as temporally related and spatially extended only because our faculties process them that way. Space and time are a priori forms of intuition, as Kant calls them.[1]

It will be appreciated how radically this view restricts our knowledge and experience. It is not only that Kant restricts factual knowledge to the data of our senses. He restricts it even more by attributing the most basic forms of sense experience to the filtering activity of the human mind. It is not Kant's view that we invent our whole world. The data of sense certainly come to us willy-nilly from beyond ourselves; but it is we who impose the manner of their appearance to ourselves – their spatio-temporal form and their most basic general characteristics as enduring and causally interacting things. The converse of this view is, as I say, complete scepticism about how things are in themselves, apart from our knowing minds.

This 'transcendental idealism', as it is called, proved highly influential in the philosophy of the post-Kantian idealists, in Schopenhauer and in Nietzsche. In more down to earth form it is to be found in the phenomenalism to which philosophers of science like Ernst Mach and many twentieth-century positivists were inclined. Its continuing hold on modern intellectuals is illustrated by Brian Magee's enthusiastic acceptance of Schopenhauer's Kantian 'insight' that we can only know things 'in the subjectively determined modes of our own perceiving and thinking and not as they are in themselves'.[2] Given Schopenhauer's great influence on modern philosophy and art – on Wagner, Wittgenstein, Proust and Thomas Mann, to name but a few of those on whom that influence has been traced – we can perhaps appreciate the pervasiveness of Kantian subjectivism and its implicit transfer of divine prerogatives to the human mind.

Kant was no atheist and I shall shortly mention the alternative route by which he himself was led to postulate God. But, once the Copernican revolution had been made and accepted, it is not surprising to find the reality of God (like that of things in themselves) becoming ever more elusive behind the screen of the human mind's own structuring of experience. We can appreciate the attractiveness of 'transcendental idealism' to atheist minds such as Nietzsche and the positivists – and indeed to the atheistic existentialists such as Sartre. The sheer Prometheanism of the modern mind – its usurpation of the place of God – and its conviction (against Kant himself) that we are the makers of our whole world, can be recognised as following ineluctably from the first step of the Copernican revolution.

A modern name for the basically Kantian view that the human mind imposes its own categorial framework on experience and thus shapes up its world in a way impossible for us to penetrate beyond is 'constructivism'. In recent philosophy, largely due to the influence of Wittgenstein, this has taken a linguistic turn – our very language being held to prescribe the limits of experience. I suggested in chapter three that this was perhaps a misunderstanding of Wittgenstein. But it remains a common conviction, at least of Anglo-Saxon, linguistic philosophy, that there is no way in which we can get outside the conceptual skin provided by our basic linguistic categories.

There is a further twist to the story of man's post-Kantian self-imprisonment within his own conceptual framework. Kant himself thought that he was spelling out the one basic conceptual scheme which all human beings necessarily employ in processing the data of sense. It is the structure of the human mind as such that yields the fundamental categories of the understanding, just as it is the structure of our faculties of sense that impose the spatio-temporal framework on all appearances. But subsequent philosophy has lost this confidence that there is only one categorial framework, common to all mankind. Kant's list of twelve basic categories[3] has come to seem somewhat arbitrary. Others have been proposed. Evidence has been cited to suggest that the list changes over time and varies from culture to culture across the globe and throughout history. Thus we reach the position known as 'conceptual relativism'. The way the world appears to us is as much the result of our own culture's way of processing the data as of the structure of the human mind. This conclusion would have horrified Kant, but it is difficult to see how it can be avoided once the notion of a given world with a knowable structure of its own has been abandoned. Constructivism leads all too easily to relativism. Complete subjectivism is only avoided by recognition of the social and cultural constraints upon the way in which any one individual represents things to himself. At best we are left with an intersubjective conception of the nature of appearances. The world as it is in itself has disappeared behind a whole set of different culturally determined screens.

It is interesting to observe how completely Cupitt has adopted this extreme consequence of the post-Kantian trend in modern philosophy. His anti-realist, expressivist understanding of religion is grafted on to a general, anti-realist, constructivist, indeed relativist view of the human 'world'. In this he is at least consistent. For, as I propose to show, once we reject this Kantian constructivism where ordinary common-sense knowledge and scientific knowledge are concerned, we are in a position to reject, indeed to refute, the suggestion that realist metaphysics and theological realism are impossible today. On the contrary, the manifest failure of constructivism to do justice either to common sense or to science leads us to question the viability of post-Kantian constructivism in any sphere of human knowledge.

Before proceeding to examine the case against a Kantian view of the limits of human knowledge and experience, we may pause to consider how Kant and some of those standing in the Kantian tradition themselves resisted the more extreme consequence of a thoroughgoing turn to the subject.

It was in the sphere of practical reason and moral philosophy that Kant himself claimed to find an antidote to the scepticism entailed by his theoretical philosophy. Indeed his avowed aim, in limiting theoretical knowledge was to make room for faith, by which he meant primarily, moral faith – the conviction that I stand inexorably under the categorical claims of the moral law. On Kant's view this is not a law imposed from outside or from above. It is a law of my own nature as a rational being. But the very fact that, as a free moral agent, I am unconditionally bound by the claims of duty shows that I transcend the limits of sense experience and theoretical understanding. Moral experience, that is to say, and moral experience alone, penetrates through the screen of appearance to the 'noumenal' world of things as they are in themselves. Admittedly Kant also thinks, for reasons that we need not explore here and which have generally been found unconvincing, that practical reason requires us to postulate God and immortality;[4] but he allows no theoretical use of these postulates. And while we ourselves might be disposed to think that there are the makings here of a moral argument for the existence of God, on the basis of which a theistic metaphysic might after all be reconstructed, Kant himself tended to move the other way, making only 'regulative' use of the idea of God and virtually translating all the doctrines of the Church into ethical terms, yielding a moral faith that certainly transcends the limits of empirical experience, but without the aid of metaphysics. It is easy to see the attraction of this stance to non-cognitivist interpreters of religion such as Cupitt; but we should recall that Kant does not regard morality as such as a purely human construct. Unlike Cupitt, Kant sees in the claims of duty, something unconditional and absolute, locating the human moral agent beyond the scope of scientific study. For Kant, the unknowableness of noumenal reality finds a necessary and all-important exception at this point.

Schopenhauer was much more Promethean than Kant in his enthusiastic espousal of the view that man's whole world, including morality, is his own idea, his project, his 'representation'. Schopenhauer was certainly an atheist. Yet, despite his Kantianism and despite his atheism, he was unable to renounce the notion of noumenal reality behind appearance, and more specifically behind the phenomena of human will and creativity. He characterises this single, undifferentiated, transcendent energy as 'will', in a sense not to be confused with our own 'phenomenal' experience of conscious willing. On the contrary, no more than Hume does Schopenhauer think of the principle behind the experienced powers of matter or mind as conscious, still less moral. The force behind all experienced representations must be thought of as pure, undifferentiated energy. It is extremely interesting to note how Schopenhauer finds clues to this transcendent will in the sexual drive and especially in art and music, though also in morality; for, like the Vedantic Hindus, Schopenhauer grounds the phenomenon of compassion in our common participation in the one undifferentiated noumenon. But it is the boundless creativity of music that most directly articulates the underlying will which Schopenhauer continues to postulate as the basic metaphysical ground of the world's being.[5]

For Kant, then, morality, and, for Schopenhauer, art, resist the purely constructivist consequences of the turn to the subject, though in each case the noumenal reality remains in itself strictly unknowable.

Other thinkers, in the Kantian tradition but against Kant's own intention, have found in religion itself a clue to the transcendent noumenal reality that grounds the whole world process. Thus Rudolf Otto speaks of the holy as an a priori category, a predisposition or impulsion of the human spirit to experience the world religiously, to respond, that is, to certain objects and occasions as both awesome and fascinating.[6] 'Numinous' experience, as Otto calls this response, is only possible because human beings are endowed with this a priori disposition. It contains both non-rational and rational elements according to Otto. It is a matter both of felt experience – the sense of the numinous – and of morality; for the rational, moral elements in developed religions serve to 'schematise' – Otto uses the Kantian terminology – the non-rational apprehension of the *mysterium trememdum et fascinans*. We have already come across an even greater emphasis on the rational element that structures religious experience in the writings of Karl Rahner,[7] who seeks to recover the whole framework of Christian doctrine as a way of articulating the necessary conditions of religious experience as such.

A fuller study of the legacy of Kant would require extended exploration of the way in which Idealist philosophers down to R. G. Collingwood have treated the phenomena of morality, art and religion, sharing the tendency I have noted to resist the purely constructivist implications of the Kantian turn to the subject. In referring to Kant's own moral philosophy, to Schopenhauer and to Otto, I have done no more than draw attention to this tendency. But of course this is only one strand in the Kantian legacy. Much more powerful have been the anti-metaphysical strands on the one hand of phenomenology and positivism, on the other of Nietzsche and Sartrean existentialism. In these movements of thought the Kantian turn to the subject has been held to involve rejection of belief in noumenal reality altogether.

The only consistent phenomenalist was in fact an unrepentant metaphysician, indeed a Christian bishop, George Berkeley. Accepting the givenness and coherence of the world of appearance, while denying the reality of a substantial objective material world to account for it, Berkeley very reasonably held that God's activity alone explained the constancy and predictability of our experience.[8] Subsequent phenomenalists and their positivist successors were less consistent and less intelligible in simply taking unexplained sense-data to constitute the building blocks of man's world.

Much more consistent, on atheist assumptions, was Nietzsche. As already noted in chapter two above, post-Kantian Prometheanism reached its apogee in Nietzsche, with his memorable declaration that 'truth is fiction'.[9] Here we encounter a thoroughly consistent atheism. With the death of God, the idea of a given world dies too. Man's world and man's values are his own free creation. So not only is there no God, and not only is there no noumenal reality transcending appearances; there is no given phenomenal world either. The phenomenal world is itself man's own project and construction.

The story of consistent atheist philosophy is very interesting to trace. It is the story of the self-destruction of the Kantian turn to the subject. Nietzschean constructivism lies behind the existentialism of Sartre. Sartre insisted that there is no discoverable human essence. We choose what we will be and we create our own values.[10] Yet the authentic human subject, creator of its own world, retains a certain absoluteness in this philosophy. The insecurity of such a stress on the human subject has become clear in French philosophy since Sartre.[11] It was first undermined by the search for hidden structures below the surface of conscious life. This 'structuralism' was a short-lived reaction. It was far too absolutist, far too reminiscent of the 'given' for thinkers steeped in the legacy of Nietzsche. In the post-structuralist thought of Michel Foucault and in the 'deconstructionism' of Jacques Derrida, atheist philosophy reaches its logical conclusion. The death of God is followed by the death of man. Man, the creator of all values, saws off the branch on which he is sitting, losing all significance in the total fragmentation of everything.

It is against this background that Cupitt's project is to be seen. Accepting, without question, Nietzsche's anti-metaphysical constructivism, Cupitt thinks that he can stem the tide of relativism and fragmentation by the purely subjective (or – to be fair – intersubjective) affirmation of Christian moral and spiritual ideals. It is hard to think that this is more than whistling in the dark.

Surveying the history of philosophy since the Kantian Copernican revolution or 'turn to the subject', we have traced its more radical atheistic consequences in the successive rejection of metaphysics, objective value, a given world, and finally the subject itself. We have also mentioned what is now a less dominant, still metaphysical, idealist reaction to Kant, finding in the presuppositions of human experience, especially moral, aesthetic and religious experience, hints of an absolute, transcendent, noumenal reality that resist the slide into nihilism.

But there are good reasons for not getting into the position in the first place, where one has to choose between the constructivist slide into nihilism and the obscure idealist recovery of the absolute via the a priori conditions of man's experience of value. There are good reasons for rejecting Kant's Copernican revolution, for refusing to set out on the path that turns the human subject into the sole source of what reality is to be for us. There simply is no need to be so sceptical about our capacity to achieve objective knowledge, not only about man but about the world and about God as well. For it is entirely reasonable to hold that the world as it is in itself is accessible to human perception and knowledge, and it is also reasonable, if not so certain, to hold that God gives himself to be known by us for what he is in himself. It follows that only in relation to a given world and a self-revealing God does man learn who and what he is.

The starting-point for a rejection of Kant's philosophy is common sense. Most people learn at an early stage that they were born into a world of a determinate nature, which existed long before there were any human beings to think about it, observe it and alter it. The world is certainly a changing world, even prior to human interference, but mountains and seas, rivers and forests and the animals and birds were and are what they are quite irrespective of man's perceptions and actions. In particular, this whole natural world into which each one of us is born is a temporally structured process and a spatially extended set of interacting systems quite apart from human knowledge. Time and space are discovered to be all-pervasive features of the way the real world is organised and its parts interrelated. This, at least, is the most plausible hypothesis, from this common-sense point of view, to account for our everyday experience.

As evolved products of this real changing world, we have presumably developed the faculties most appropriate for living successfully in it, including the sense organs and conceptual apparatus most suited to intelligent awareness of the nature of the world in which we find ourselves, and of ourselves as part of that world. As I say, prior to any further scientific refinement of our knowledge of the world, we find it to be a relatively stable planet, composed of relatively enduring physical substances, productive of relatively stable natural kinds – animal, vegetable and mineral – all enduring through time and spatially related to each other.

The faculties that yield cognitive awareness of the world are, as Kant rightly says, those of sense and understanding. But it is foolish to treat either the data of sense or the concepts of the understanding as though they are themselves the objects of our awareness. On the contrary, they are the media or vehicles of our perceptual awareness of things. The fact that a complex causal interaction takes place between ourselves and the world, and the fact that an even more complex sorting and ordering process takes place in the brain and mind – a process that only occurs easily and automatically after much education and learning – in no way cut us off from the world. On the contrary, they are the acquired and learned mechanisms of perceptual awareness of a world which exists with the properties and powers we perceive quite independently of us.

So far, I have mentioned only the animal, vegetable and mineral substances of the world process and the natural kinds they compose, of which we become aware. But of course the human world increasingly consists of artefacts and a culturally created environment, whose meaning *does* depend on human projects and intentions. But although a knife does not possess its status and significance as a knife apart from human purposes, it is certainly a physical object, existing in space and time, and endowed with physical properties which would remain what they are even if all human beings were eliminated. The same is true of all buildings in a city and all books on library shelves. I admit that it is an entirely reasonable, common-sense supposition – though we shall have theological reasons for questioning it later – that all *meaning* would disappear from a world without human beings. But the artefacts themselves would remain.

This common-sense view of the independent reality of substances and of natural and artificial objects, far from being undermined by modern science, is confirmed by it. Science extends our awareness of the world about us beyond its perceptual base to an astonishing degree. Physics and cosmology extend our knowledge of the space-time structure of the cosmos back to unimaginable conditions within seconds of the hot 'big bang' and across unimaginable distances as vast numbers of galaxies rush away from each other at speeds approaching that of light. The idea that space and time are not inherent relational characteristics of the universe, irrespective of human observers, is quite incredible to the working scientist.

Our knowledge of the properties and composition of things is also greatly extended by the sciences, from biology down to (or up to) elementary particle physics. But all this fascinating information about elementary particles, energies, forces and fields, and about the chemical elements and their modes of combination that make the emergence of life possible at a late stage in cosmic evolution, in no way entails the unreality of the perceived properties and powers of relatively large-scale objects, natural and artificial, of which ordinary everyday perception and activity make us aware. We realise, rather, that the perceived properties of things are only some of their properties. But perceived and unperceived properties and powers are all equally real and equally what they are, irrespective of our knowing minds.

There are two last-ditch ways of defending a Kantian, constructivist view of modern science. One stems from recognition of the observer's inescapable role in quantum physics. In sub-atomic particle physics, it seems that we reach a theoretically uncrossable threshold where any conceivable method of observation would necessarily alter what is being observed. But this does not prevent the physicist from postulating real, perhaps random interactions underlying and explaining the behaviour of the basic building-blocks of matter. Only the incurably positivist mind jibs at the postulation of theoretically unobservable entities and energies.

The other argument stems from one way of interpreting the so-called 'anthropic principle', which traces back into the early stages of cosmic evolution the conditions rendering the emergence of life, consciousness and mind possible, even inevitable. The constructivist way of interpreting this is to see it as an inevitable projection back by intelligent creatures of the conditions that make their presence itself intelligible. But this is a highly implausible way of taking the anthropic principle. In the next chapter I shall argue that the striking initial conditions in the hot 'big bang' which made possible the evolution of life and mind at a later stage in cosmic evolution cannot possibly be regarded as a figment of our imagination. On the contrary, when we consider what was and what must have been the case if life and mind were ever to evolve, we shall find that we have the basis for a serious design argument for the existence of God.

Indeed, in chapter seven I shall argue further that our manifest ability to find out the truth about the world around us, whether through everyday engagement with it or through scientific theory and research, belies the Nietzschean claim that 'truth is fiction' – the alleged consequence of the 'death of God' – and enables us rather to construct an argument from manifest truth to its only secure explanation in the creative will of God.

All that is to anticipate. My purpose here, in sketching what I hope is a critical (rather than naive), realist view of the world, is simply to show that there is no need to set out on the Kantian constructivist path where our knowledge of the external world is concerned. In no way are we cut off from the real world by our senses and concepts. Rather they present real features of the world to us that are only refined and supplemented in science. Least of all need we doubt that spatial extension and temporal relation are real features of the world, quite apart from ourselves.

Now, if we can regain confidence in the independent reality of the everyday world in which we find ourselves and in the objectivity of what the sciences disclose, and thus resist the constructivism of much post-Kantian philosophy, it is not unreasonable for us also to look again at the worlds of meaning and value which, I admitted just now, can appear to down-to-earth common sense as no more than human projects and constructions. Untrammelled by Kantian doubts about truth and the objectivity of the external world, we may be more willing to look again at those spheres of morality, art and religion, which the Kantians themselves, at least in the nineteenth and early twentieth centuries, were inclined to regard as more than purely phenomenal. Moreover, we can do so in a much more direct way than the Kantians could, given our greater confidence in the human mind's capacity to achieve objectivity. For, after all, on a realist view, cosmic evolution has, as a matter of fact, produced intelligent organisms capable not only of perception and thought but also of morality, art and religion. We cannot rest content simply with an objective account of the material universe. For it is this same material universe that has, on any reckoning, given birth to the world of the spirit as we encounter it in man. Hence the entirely rational desire, exemplified by the writers mentioned in chapter four, to give an account of our experience as a whole and to integrate scientific knowledge with what we know of man's inner world, his self-transcendence and his creativity, as these come to expression in morality, art and religion.

6

The grounds of theistic belief

I now attempt to state the case for belief in an objective God, notwithstanding the pressures against theistic metaphysics that have come to the fore in the modern period. Such arguments have both a negative and a positive thrust. Negatively, it needs to be pointed out how weak and implausible are the naturalistic alternatives available today. Positively, it needs to be shown that salient features of our experience, in this as in any age, point in the direction of God and suggest theism as the most plausible world view. Of course the negative and the positive arguments are correlated. It is the same factors that show up the weakness of naturalism and suggest or validate theism.

That, incidentally, is why there is something extremely odd in the common preference in Protestant and Catholic writing today – one thinks of Plantinga and Küng in this respect – for negative over positive apologetic. The idea that arguments *against* naturalism may clear the way to faith while arguments *for* the existence of God are somehow religiously improper is incoherent. Certainly faith is more than intellectual assent. But faith is undoubtedly assisted in its dispute with unbelief by positive natural theology. Moreover, if positive and negative arguments are two sides of the same coin, then both aspects should be welcomed. There is no reason for religious minds to be coy about this.

I reserve for the next chapter a particularly powerful

argument from truth to God. This will take as its starting point the collapse of the notion of objective truth which tends to follow the so-called 'death of God'. It is an argument particularly appropriate to the rebuttal of Cupitt's position, since it is precisely the post-Enlightenment cultural pressures welcomed by Cupitt that lead to the collapse of any serious conception of objective truth. In this chapter, however, I concentrate on arguments that have some force in any age and in any cultural setting.

One further remark by way of preface to these considerations of natural theology is worth making. The above-mentioned suspicion of arguments for the existence of God is associated not only with a particular view of faith but also with the more general suspicion of 'foundationalism' in philosophy. As pointed out in chapter four, foundationalism is the view that human knowledge, to be secure, has to be built up piece by piece on indubitable premises, the whole structure being no more reliable than its sure foundations. This view, which has dominated western theory of knowledge since Descartes, is widely criticised today by supporters of more 'holistic' theories of meaning and truth, which see the rationality of human knowledge much more in terms of the internal coherence of a whole systematic way of looking at the world than in terms of a view supported step by step by a series of indubitable arguments going back to absolutely bedrock certainties. There is much to be said for such holistic theories and indeed I shall be arguing that the internal rationality of a developed theistic belief system is one of the major factors in its favour. But, given the variety of religious and philosophical views to be found in the world, it seems unreasonable to rule out the quest for some good arguments in favour of one way of construing things rather than another. Such external supporting arguments do not have to take the form of indubitable, demonstrative proofs. They are much more likely to stem from pretty tentative reflections on a number of factors, poorly accounted for in purely naturalistic theories, which perhaps only when taken together in a broadly cumulative case, can be seen to give support to a religious view of the world, and to make belief in God more probably true.

What are these factors? What is it that a naturalistic view (whether secular or 'religious' in Cupitt's sense) leaves out of account? In the first place, we should face, fairly and squarely, the problem of ultimate explanation. Any purely naturalistic view – and Cupitt's is no exception – leaves the very existence of the world quite unexplained. This problem is not to be confused with the even more basic wonder that can strike us human beings at the existence of anything at all, God included. An absolutely necessary being would still excite wonder at its being there, but, since there would be no question of its not being there, no way in which it might have come into being or go out of being, and no question of its being, in essence, other than it is, the question why it is there at all could get no purchase hold. We have to assume that an absolutely necessary being is self-explanatory in a way no other being is, even if we cannot see the inner logic, so to speak, of its self-explanatoriness. Now naturalists sometimes suggest that, for all we know, the world itself – the universe – may be that absolutely necessary being. (At other times they make the very different suggestion that the world is just a brute fact, which no one is in a position to explain. Explanations, they say, are only possible within the system, which we can do no other than take without question as the framework within which to explain things. This seems pretty arbitrary. The quest for explanation cannot be halted just like that.) The trouble with the suggestion that the universe itself may be the absolutely necessary being is its extreme implausibility given the very precise nature of the stuff of which it is made and of the laws which govern its processes. The 'contingency' of the universe consists in its being just so and not otherwise, when, for all we can tell, it might have been otherwise. Indeed, cosmologists sometimes speculate that the laws of nature may be different in other parts of the universe or that there are perhaps infinitely many universes, each different in its substance, structure and laws from this one. That seems to me to concede the contingency of the universe which we inhabit and allow us to press the question why. Admittedly, it is less easy to press this question if our universe is one of an infinite number of universes. Perhaps the infinite totality of universes is the absolutely necessary being which our quest for explanation seeks. But it is far from clear that the postulation of an infinite number of existing universes is a more plausible or more simple explanation than attributing this universe to the deliberate creation of an absolutely necessary God.

It should be stressed that what we are seeking in this kind of metaphysical exploration is the explanation of this universe's existence. We seek the cause of its being in being. This is a very different kind of cause from the causal explanations sought in science. *Given* the basic substance and laws of nature, we can seek scientific explanations of processes and phenomena within the system. But that in no way explains why the system is there in the first place. It is the contingency of the system – its being just so, when as far as we can see it could have been different – that makes us seek the cause, in the metaphysical sense, of its being in being.

So the first problem in any kind of naturalism is its complete failure to offer any explanation at all of why the world exists. Of course, the absolutely necessary being posited to account for the world's being is not, at this stage in the argument, characterised in any religiously satisfying way. It is simply the absolutely necessary ground of the contingent universe's being. But if there are other reasons for believing in God, it is quite plausible to equate the metaphysician's absolute with the God of religion. For no developed religion will rest content with a contingent God, about whom further why questions will inevitably arise.

The metaphysician himself may also feel the force of the suggestion that it is simpler and more intelligible to attribute the universe's being just so and not otherwise to an absolute *intention* rather than to a mindless absolute. Explicit intention for good reasons is perhaps the most intelligible and satisfying explanation of anything. The force of this argument, however, is hard to assess when taken by itself apart from further considerations stemming from the actual nature of the world in which we live.

Much the most powerful general argument for the existence of God is the design argument. This takes as its starting point not the bare existence of a contingent world, nor even the fact of the world's being an orderly affair, but rather the quite astonishing kind of order manifested by the world's capacity to evolve living, conscious, rational and personal beings. A modern design argument does not begin with particular phenomena such as the eye or the brain and claim that such complex things bespeak design. On the contrary, given the nature of fundamental particles and their capacity to combine into atomic, molecular and organic structures, the theory of evolution can to a large extent – though perhaps not wholly – explain the development of living forms. That is an example of scientific explanation within a given system. What is not explained is the system itself and its power to produce such things as life and mind. The suggestion that an explicit intention lies behind the whole process finds much support from recent cosmological discoveries, notably from discovery of the extreme specificity and narrowness of range in the conditions following the 'big bang' if life and mind were ever to have the chance of evolving at a later stage in the history of the universe. We now know that, had conditions been fractionally different from what they were, all matter would either have turned into hydrogen and helium or collapsed in on itself again, in neither case leaving time and space for the formation of the chemical elements necessary to the evolution of life. The basic stuff (and mass) of the universe and the fundamental laws of nature are therefore required to be just what they are if galactic, solar and planetary systems are to form, in which life and mind can evolve.

Once again the naturalistic mind is forced to go to extraordinary lengths to concoct alternative theories to that of design in order to account for the facts just indicated. The 'multiple universe' theory is called upon again to suggest that perhaps there exist innumerable universes, in which every permutation of the basic energies is gone through, and we exist in the one which happened to get the conditions right for the later emergence of life and mind. Apart from my previous point that this in principle, unverifiable theory seems more extravagant than theism itself, it can also be urged that it still fails to account for the basic facts that form the starting point of the design argument. For even if the stuff of the world goes through an endless series of permutations, it still possesses the capacity, sooner or later, to combine in such a way as to produce life and mind. It is this capacity which remains entirely unexplained, whether it takes one run or many trial runs for the conditions to obtain in which that capacity can be realised. Design explains that capacity – and, of course, given design, the multiple universe theory becomes redundant.

So the second problem in any kind of naturalism is its complete failure to account for the capacity of elementary particles or energies under the fundamental laws of nature, to evolve and combine in such a way as to produce life and mind. Again, by this route alone we can hardly claim to discern the God of religion, still less the God of Christian faith. By itself, the design argument cannot even establish the infinity or absolute necessity of the mind behind the cosmic process. That is why the cosmological and the design arguments have to be taken together. But the design argument does strongly reinforce the suggestion that it is most intelligible to posit *intention* as the ultimate explanation for the world's being there. For the nature of the world – its mind-producing capacity, especially where the initial conditions of the production of finite minds have to be so precise – is clearly indicative of intention. Even so, the postulation of an infinite mind behind the world's being and nature can at best have only a supportive role when it comes to defending belief in the objective God of Christian faith.

The design argument's postulation of deliberate intention behind the world process is open to very grave counter arguments, however, stemming from the problem of evil. Of course, we have not yet seen reason to attribute moral qualities such as benevolence and love to the intelligent world cause. When such reasons are given, as they will be given subsequently in this chapter, the graveness of the problem of evil is doubly underlined. But already it may seem quite incoherent to postulate design when so much about the human world appears to manifest lack of design or sheer incompetence. As Hume put it, the whole world may give the impression of 'a blind nature, impregnated by a great vivifying principle, and pouring forth from her lap, without discernment or parental care, her maimed and abortive children'.[1] Some solution to the problem of evil is therefore required before the force of the design argument can be fully appreciated. Of course, the facts suggestive of design remain – it is still a great mystery how the world process can have it in it to produce rational beings – but if a solution to the problem of evil could be found, if, that is, it could be shown how any finite world capable of producing persons is bound to be vulnerable to suffering and at risk to moral evil, then the design argument would retain its full force in the cumulative case for belief in an objective God.

A solution to the problem of evil must contain much more than the so-called 'free-will defence', whereby the possibility of wrong choice and of the corruption of the will is seen to be of the essence of finite personhood, at least in its formative stages. For it is the necessities of that formation – the building up of finite life and personhood from below, in and through a regularly structured physical universe – which explain the susceptibility of finite persons both to accident (including disaster) and to temptation. Such a theodicy cannot be developed here.[2] I simply indicate its necessity at this stage in the argument.

The next group of considerations suggestive of objective theism is to be found in the very phenomenon of man – that finite, rational and personal being who has, as a matter of fact, evolved through cosmic and biological evolution, and who, as far as we know, represents the highest point so far of complexification in the history of the cosmos. (If there are more advanced rational beings in the universe, then doubtless they could enhance the argument. But there is no evidence of this.) Here we come to the anthropological considerations, already touched on in our survey of modern theology in chapter four in connection with writers such as Pannenberg, Macquarrie and Rahner. It is very difficult to account, on purely naturalistic principles, for man's freedom, his openness to the future, his self-transcendence and creativity, and his perception and espousal of aesthetic, moral and religious values.

Value will itself shortly be cited as a further starting point for a group of 'axiological'[3] arguments for the existence of God. Here we concentrate on the anthropological argument from man's freedom and creativity to God as their source. For not only are freedom and creativity hard to explain 'from below' by reference to what has crudely been called 'bottom-up' causality (which finds it impossible to avoid a highly implausible, deterministic account of man); they are also

93

positively suggestive of a 'top-down' final causality whereby the creature is drawn out of nature into spirit by and from the world of spirit itself.[4]

Moreover man's fundamental trust in reality (Küng), his sense that the universe that has produced him is not, ultimately speaking, alien but rather a home, is much more explicable on a theistic than on a naturalistic view. When this consideration is taken together with the design argument from the universe's capacity to produce such a self-transcending creature as man, then the greater reasonableness of taking mind to be the clue to the ultimate nature of things over taking it to be no more than 'a little agitation of the brain'[5] becomes apparent.

These general anthropological arguments are greatly enhanced by consideration of the values which human beings come to perceive in the world about them and in their own intersubjective existence as persons in relation. I am thinking here primarily of the values of beauty, moral goodness and love. Arguments from value to the existence of God (axiological arguments) take as their premise the fact that the universe contains these values. We find or create things (and scenes) of surpassing beauty. Human beings can and do manifest transparent moral goodness. Human capacity for interpersonal relation reaches its highest expression in the four forms of love – affection, the mutuality of friendship, the ecstasy of sexual love, and the other-regarding, sometimes self-sacrificial love of the neighbour in his need (extending, in principle, to every human being as a potential neighbour). These values constitute the most striking and significant phenomena in the world. How is their presence to be explained?

There has been much debate over the subjectivity or objectivity of value. The beauty of nature, though it takes human subjects to appreciate it, cannot plausibly be held to lie solely in the eye of the beholder. Even the beauty of works of art – unquestionably constructed as they are by human beings – in large part depends on the natural substances of which those works are made and the natural forms which they often represent. We create beautiful things but we do not create beauty. Moreover we, the appreciators and creators of beautiful things, are ourselves products of nature. There are senses, then, in which aesthetic values are objective, are there in the nature of things. Moral values too, as phenomena here on earth, are clearly dependent on there being human beings to recognise and exemplify them, and yet they are most implausibly thought of as nothing but subjective preferences. Moral goodness and love are in large part constituted by acceptance of the *claims* which human beings make on each other simply by being here. The moral universe is not an arbitrary creation of the human will – nor even of human society over time. Human nature itself, though a product of cosmic and biological evolution, is inescapably moral. There is a sense, then, in which moral values, too, are objective, are there in the nature of things.

Just as the capacity of the universe to produce minds led us to postulate an intention behind the cosmic process, so the capacity of the universe to produce beauty, goodness and love leads us to suppose that these values reflect an ultimate source of value, itself supremely valuable. For it is very hard to see how elementary particles and energies and fields of force, operating solely with 'bottom-up' efficient causality, can by themselves account for the values which human beings perceive and exemplify.

Among the phenomena of human life and experience which may plausibly be held to point to a transcendent source of being and value, pride of place must be given to the phenomenon of religion itself, and especially to the widespread, if not universal, phenomenon of theism, of belief in, and alleged experience of, the divine. Throughout recorded history and all over the globe we find examples of such belief and experience – in primitive monotheism among many tribal peoples as in Africa, in the ancient polytheistic cults, in the developed world religions of East and West. Judaism, Christianity and Islam, devotional Hinduism, Sikhism and many other faiths have given religious and sometimes philosophical expression to a sense of God that takes the form sometimes of awe and abasement before a transcendent source of being and value, and sometimes of felt union with the spirit immanent in everything. The classical Roman poet, Lucretius, in his *De Rerum Natura*, Hume in the eighteenth century, and many nineteenth and early twentieth-century anthropologists and psychologists have attempted to give naturalistic, reductionist explanations of this common human phenomenon of alleged experience of God as being grounded in fear of the unknown, wish-fulfilment, projection or whatever. The task of negative apologetic, as in Küng's *Does God Exist?* or in John Bowker's *The Sense of God*,[6] is to show up the poverty and implausibility of these reductionist explanations. Those who have themselves enjoyed religious experience of God are seldom convinced for a moment by the reductionists. Neutral observers of the human scene will be likely to be more or less impressed by the fact and prevalence of such alleged experience of God in proportion to their conviction or lack of conviction of the force of the previously mentioned arguments, cosmological, teleological, anthropological and axiological. To anyone persuaded of even some probabilistic force in the accumulation of these rational arguments, the fact of religious experience, interpreted as experience of God, will hardly come as a surprise. Indeed it stands to reason that if there is, as these arguments suggest, a transcendent source of the world's being and nature and of the values that have emerged in the course of the long cosmic process, then we should expect that transcendent reality to be encounterable experientially by human subjects who are the products of the world process.

Indeed it is only reasonable further to expect some revelation from the mind and will behind the process. Thus to anyone, even half persuaded by the arguments, the very fact of world religion can have a confirming effect. Much greater confirmation will of course be found if the observer himself enjoys what seems to him to be an experience or experiences of God.

However, the way in which religion complements the arguments and yields a belief in God that is experientially as well as rationally based is not simply a question of matching the public arguments with some private religious experience. The world religions have provided, down the centuries, traditions of interpreting religious experience that claim to be responses to divine revelation – revelation not in the sense of a private disclosure to an individual, a prophet, for example, or a sage – but rather in the sense of public objective revelation, channelled through a book, through a series of historical events, or through the story of an alleged divine incarnation. It is these traditions of revelation and response that give some specificity and knowability to the God of religion. Revealed theology fills out natural theology's concept of necessary ground, designer, and source of value, with, for example, the concept of the trinitarian God of love, allegedly revealed through Jesus Christ and the gift of the Spirit. And just as the rational arguments of natural theology encourage us to take the fact of religious experience seriously as a source of our knowledge of God, so those same arguments encourage us to take revelation claims seriously as given and valid ways of construing the world and experience religiously.

Something will be said in chapter nine about the problem of the diversity of world religions. Certainly any one developed form of theism, say that of Christianity, will have to include a plausible account of religion the world over and of the differences as well as the things in common between itself and other forms of theism. But a developed theistic religion, grounded, allegedly, in divine revelation, can be articulated theologically in very powerful and far-reaching ways. Some indication of creative, modern, Christian, natural theology has already been given in chapter four. The point to be stressed now is that those same theologians have gone on to spell out Christianity's revelation-based theology in terms of a total world view that is intellectually as well as morally and spiritually very persuasive. This is what I meant by the appeal to the inner rationality of a Christian systematic theology that offers, in the doctrines of Creation, Incarnation, Redemption and the Kingdom of God, a total interpretation of existence. It is in this connection that the more holistic theories of meaning and truth can be welcomed by the Christian apologist. For it is the total interconnected scheme of interpretation of the world and of human life, summed up in Christian doctrine and explored in Christian theology that, according to Christian faith, gives specific content as well as much greater power of conviction to the vague ideas of God that come from natural theology or religious experience.

The case for belief in an objective God, therefore, consists in an accumulation of diverse considerations. We appeal in the first place to very general features of the world – its existence and rational order, its capacity to produce intelligent, self-transcending beings and the values of beauty, goodness and love. We appeal to the widespread sense of God that comes to expression in religious experience the world over. And we appeal to the light thrown on everything by a fully developed Christian understanding of God and the world. Far from pulling in different directions, these appeals reinforce each other and yield rational support for a faith by which to live. Moreover, the rational support does not only come from the natural theology defended here. The appeal to experience – to the widespread fact of religious experience and to one's own religious experience if one has had it – and the appeal to revealed theology's own inner rationality in making most sense of everything – are perfectly rational appeals as well.

Consequently, there is no clash between the God of philosophy and the God of religion. It is the very same God, dimly apprehended through the philosophical arguments of natural theology as the source and goal of all there is, who is also self-disclosed in Christ as the God of love evoking the religious response of gratitude and dedication. Alternatively, it might be better to say that there is no such thing as the God of philosophy. There is only the God of religion. For religion yields a closer, more 'real' (in Newman's terminology) apprehension of the very same ultimate reality of which philosophy gives us some 'notional' intimation.

I will conclude these reflections on the grounds of theistic belief by referring again to the intellectual poverty of secular naturalism, taken over without question by Cupitt as the presupposition of a purely expressivist and voluntarist religion.

The late J. L. Mackie, in his posthumously published *The Miracle of Theism*,[7] subjected the arguments for the existence of God to a sustained critical analysis, wholly negative in its outcome. On close inepction, however, Mackie's objections can be seen to carry little weight. His treatment of the cosmological argument, for example, simply does not face up to the problematic nature of a contingent universe consisting of just such energy and mass, governed by just such fundamental laws. On the design argument, he allows that 'some small variation from the actual initial materials and constants would perhaps eliminate the possibility of life's having developed as it did'. But his only comment is that, since we have no idea of what other interesting possibilities might have been latent within others of the endless range of possible initial conditions 'we are not in a position . . . to regard the actual initial materials and constants as a uniquely fruitful set, and as surprising and as specially calling for further explanation on that account'.[8] This is a very weak reply. Given the actual nature of matter or energy, any variation in the actual conditions following the 'big bang' would quite clearly not have permitted any form of life at all to appear at a later stage. There are no interesting possibilities in a universe consisting of nothing but hydrogen and helium or of nothing but gravitational collapse.

Mackie's objection to arguments from value may be illustrated by his brief treatment of moral arguments for the existence of God. Here he relies on the bare assertion that 'we can find satisfactory biological, sociological and psychological explanations of moral thinking which account for the phenomena of the moral sense and conscience in natural terms'.[9] Similarly he just asserts that all religious experience can be explained on purely natural grounds. Against Küng, he says that nihilism is countered not by a rationally justified fundamental trust in reality, but by the *invention* of value. There is a quite extraordinary confidence here in man's ability to face the threat of meaninglessness by his own construction of a moral universe.

Not only does Mackie show no sense of wonder at the presence in the world of beauty, goodness and love, his naturalistic assumptions also lead him into a positive disparagement of the phenomenon of man – man's mind and rationality and, most strikingly of all, man's freedom. In his treatment of the problem of evil, Mackie rebuts the 'free-will defence' by what amounts to a denial of freedom. Everything, we are told, could be and probably is determined. Even the Naxi Holocaust was the result of situations in which the German people had got trapped.[10] It was no one's fault. Correlatively we must assume that, for Mackie, the whole world of value is not *freely* invented but rather is itself a kind of defence mechanism on the part of narrower or wider groups determined by their relative needs.

In his treatment of value, it has to be admitted that Mackie is in a sense more consistent than Cupitt. A consistent naturalism is bound to try to reduce value to a human product rather than a free creative invention. Cupitt's existentialist espousal of human freedom and creativity in the positing of moral and spiritual worlds rests much less easily upon the anti-metaphysical, naturalistic assumptions that he shares with Mackie. Against both there needs to be set the kind of case sketched here for the greater rationality of theistic belief.

One further point against Mackie may be added. In his discussion of natural evil, Mackie shows an extraordinary blindness to the *logical* force of the kind of 'Irenaean' theodicies advanced by such writers as Tennant and Hick.[11] If rootedness in a regularly structured evolving world is a *logically* necessary condition of the realisation of the values of human personhood, then it is no limit on omnipotence to be unable to avoid the *inherent* risks in such a creative process.

7
The question of truth

The issue at stake between voluntarists and realists in religion is a question of truth. The voluntarist argues (or assumes) that it is not true that there exists an objective God, Creator of heaven and earth. The realist, by contrast, argues – along the lines, for example, of the last two chapters – that belief in an objective God is true. Another way of putting the difference is to say that, for the voluntarist or expressivist, religious truth is not a matter of stating, as far as human language can, how things ultimately are and will be with God, man and the world, but rather a matter simply of how one lives and of what ideals guide one's policies, commitments and choices. This point is sometimes made – very confusedly – by saying that the word 'true' means something different in talk of God from what it means in talk of tables and chairs and the people in the room.

Undoubtedly, talk of God is very different from talk of chairs and people, and of course it is religiously and theologically essential to bring out the differences. But there is no need, indeed it is quite improper, to make the concept of truth a victim of these differences and to suppose that an expressivist or voluntarist view of religious language allows us to mean by the *truth* of God no more than the value of one's highest ethical and spiritual ideal. On the contrary, truth is first and foremost a property of statements or beliefs which they possess when things are as they state or hold them to be.

Moreover the words 'true' and 'false' retain precisely the same meaning whatever we are talking about, however great the differences between the various objects of discourse.

This is the sense in which it is claimed here that the issue at stake is a question of truth: is it *true* that God exists objectively (and consequently *false* that the word 'God' denotes no more than an intersubjective ideal)? A further issue, to be discussed in the final chapter, is whether the Christian Church is committed to their being an objective God, in this metaphysically realist sense. The vast majority of Christians and all representative Church bodies hold that it is so committed.

But clearly the prior and primary issue is the truth or falsity of the belief that God exists. In the previous chapter a number of reasons were given for thinking it to be true that God does indeed exist as the source and goal of all there is, the mind behind the cosmos and the absolute ground of value. In this chapter, I want to show how closely bound up with the truth of God's existence is the question of truth in general. In fact I want to explore a further argument for God's existence, namely the argument from truth to God.

The history of western thought since the Enlightenment has revealed how vulnerable the concept of truth in general is to loss of belief in God. Nietzsche's aphorism that when God is dead, truth becomes fiction, is not nearly as extravagant a notion as it at first appears. Chapter five traced the story of that major, post-Kantian strand in modern thought that ascribes more and more of man's world to an increasingly diverse set of socially determined human constructions. The notion of reality as it is in itself, prior to human experience and knowing becomes ever more elusive. It was pointed out how twentieth-century modernity has seen in existentialism, structuralism and post-structuralism, further movements in an ever more arbitrary direction, now breaking up even the *socially* constructed norms which at first succeeded the old idea of objective truth. The project of 'deconstruction' associated with the name of the French philosopher, Jacques Derrida,[1] shows how fragile is the fabric of modernity. Yet he has nothing to put in its place. These trends are reflected in much modern art, which demonstrates the emptiness and arbitrariness of a sensibility bereft of contact with the real.

Many minds, including many non-religious minds, instinctively resist these trends. Common-sense conviction that the world about us consists of things and kinds of things that are what they are prior to and quite apart from any observation and thought, and are discovered to be what they are by the learned and self-correcting use of fallible human faculties, is a conviction that for the most part survives sceptical assault. It survives too the kind of scientific assault that bases itself on the vast range of unobservable properties of things discovered in the natural sciences; for whatever else things are, for the most part they remain what common sense has always taken them to be as well. And it survives the kind of philosophical assault that bases itself on recognition of the prevalence of different conceptual schemes, the 'theory-laden' nature of perception, and the 'underdetermination of theory' by the data of our senses;[2] for regular human practical engagement with the world about us easily eliminates the many far-fetched though possible ways of construing the data that philosophical sceptics like to suggest.

It is quite proper to include human beings in the list of natural kinds that are what they are prior to and quite apart from any observation and thought. I do not deny that, with the arrival of *homo sapiens* on the evolutionary scene, whole new classes of partly, indeed heavily, mind-dependent realities – artefacts, cultures, the whole hugely variegated human world – supervene upon the natural world. But it would be a mistake to list only the mineral, vegetable and animal natural kinds that long pre-existed the appearance of *homo sapiens*. For man is a product of natural evolution, and people have a natural structure and form more basic than any cultural or social overlaying and should, therefore, be included in the list of what there is, irrespective of the mind's constructions.

This common-sense realism, far from being incompatible with science, is in fact only extended and confirmed by science. For, on the one hand, scientific research greatly supplements our everyday perceptions of the world, including ourselves; and, on the other hand, by explaining the interconnections of things and uncovering more and more of the properties and powers particularly of material substances, it enables us to weed out from our pre-scientific picture of the world, the primitive superstitions and ill-informed guesses that undoubtedly marred the common-sense view of earlier generations.

Admittedly, the theories in terms of which the natural sciences expand and systematise our knowledge of the world are partial, provisional and revisable human constructions. So, for that matter, are the human languages themselves in which we formulate and express both our common sense and our scientific understanding of the world. Yet the function of both language and scientific theory is to articulate and advance awareness of what there is – first and foremost of what there is in any case, quite apart from human knowledge and human interests.

Moreover, even the human worlds of artefacts and culture and interests depend to a greater extent on what there is irrespective of those, largely social constructions. Thus a hammer can only be what it is in human purposive activity because of the properties and powers of wood and iron; a Gothic cathedral depends on the properties of stone and glass; and the institution of marriage is related to the biological facts and needs of human generation and nurture.

Common sense and natural science, then, are strongly suggestive of metaphysical realism. We discover, by experience of the world about us and by interaction with it, what there is and what it is like. The vast majority of ordinary people and the vast majority of working scientists remain convinced that they are exploring at least a wide range of the manifest and hidden features of an objective universe, and that the beliefs and affirmations which they hold or make about what they find are, however approximately, true.

Despite the aforementioned philosophical tendency, since Descartes and Kant and especially since Nietzsche, to question and doubt such metaphysical realism, there remain a number of secular, even physicalist philosophers who defend the view of objectivity and truth sketched here. One such philosopher is Anthony Quinton in *The Nature of Things*.[3] Another is the Australian philosopher, Michael Devitt, who, in his *Realism and Truth*,[4] defends metaphysical realism against several leading proponents of anti-realism. He argues, for example, against the philosopher of science, Bas Van Fraassen, who is sceptical about unobservable entities, that we *can* learn about objects that affect us indirectly just as readily as we can about observables. If the postulation of unobservable entities enables us to explain what we see (say, in bubble chambers or on television screens) better than any other theory, then that is a good reason for believing that those unobservable entities exist. Devitt argues against the radical subjectivist philosophers of science, Thomas Kuhn and Paul Feuerabend, that their views make nonsense of progress in science and of the confirmation or disconfirmation of theories, most implausible of all being their scepticism over our ability to *refer* to what exists quite independently of ourselves. Again the postulation of independent objects of reference *explains* things far better than any other hypothesis. Similarly, Devitt argues powerfully against Donald Davidson's scepticism over reference, on

106

account of its implausible denial of any reality apart from and independent of our various conceptual schemes. It makes nonsense of our experience to suppose that our conceptual schemes prevent us from referring to realities as they are in themselves rather than enabling us to do just that.

Most trenchantly of all, Devitt marshals his arguments against what he calls 'the renegade Putnam'. The philosopher, Hilary Putnam, for many years a staunch defender of metaphysical realism, latterly abandoned that view in favour of what he calls 'internalist' realism, whereby 'the mind and the world jointly make up the mind and the world'. What brought about this shift in Putnam's views was a growing conviction that interest determines our explanations and that there is no way in which we can get outside the conceptual scheme in terms of which we construe the real. Against this Devitt argues again that the postulation of reality, independent of the human mind, provides a better explanation of the facts of our experience than the internalist view. Finally, he argues against Michael Dummett's anti-realism (which requires a verificationist theory of meaning and truth, whereby what is to count as true *depends* on our all-too-human means of testing any claim) that there are just too many difficulties with this latter view for it to be allowed to overthrow the presumption, from common sense and science, in favour of realism and an understanding of truth as correspondence between our beliefs and how things are.

So we are faced with the intriguing situation in which common sense, working science, and a number of contemporary philosophers such as Quinton and Devitt are to be found, with great plausibility, resisting the anti-realist, constructivist tendencies that we have seen in much post-Nietzschean, continental and analytic philosophy, to follow the so-called 'death of God'. It is at this point that we can begin to sketch our argument from truth to God. For such a robust, common-sense realism and the conception of objective truth that goes with it, undoubtedly represent a vulnerable stance, if merely asserted without metaphysical support. It is vulnerable on two scores. In the first place, realism of the kind advocated by Devitt, while plausible from the standpoints both of common sense and practical science, remains entirely unaccounted for. The properties and powers of basic matter or energy and its concretion, under highly specific and constant laws into the natural kinds which we observe around us, are accepted simply as brute facts by realists such as Devitt. The objectivity of the natural world is accepted and affirmed, but it is unexplained. In the second place, Devitt's metaphysical realism is vulnerable in that he also affirms a purely physicalist or materialist account of consciousness and the human mind. Certainly he holds that realism is one thing, physicalism another. But, unlike realism, physicalism is an implausible doctrine. It fails to do justice to the phenomena of consciousness, let alone mental life and experience. Such espousal of physicalism by realists such as Devitt is, of course, an indication of a willingness to let natural science prevail over common sense in the philosophy of mind. But part of the strength of the realist position is its robust common sense. Certainly there are cases where we do and must allow science to correct common sense. Early examples concerned the roundness of the earth and its moving round the sun. But a physicalist account of mind and its products is as implausible as a constructivist account of the natural world. Common-sense realism very properly includes realism about thoughts, experiences and their subjects, and also about the whole of what Karl Popper has called 'World 3', namely, the products of the human mind, including art, religion and philosophy.[5]

These two vulnerabilities – the unexplained character of objectivity and the implausible reductionism which physicalism entails – render a metaphysical realism of the sort espoused by Devitt somewhat insecure, notwithstanding its manifest common sense and scientific plausibility over against the anti-realist, constructivist tendencies of much post-Enlightenment modernity. Moreover, as we have seen, it remains vulnerable, in an atheistic context, to Nietzschean erosion. The argument now to be explored attempts to remove these insecurities by grounding both the objectivity of nature and its capacity to produce minds and the world of mind in an objective God, whose creative will explains both the objectivity of things and the fact that the universe includes minds. That this is an argument and not the bare assertion of a theistic world view is shown by the facts that it starts from the objectivity of the natural world (its specific substance and laws and the natural kinds that have evolved), proceeds by showing the implausibility of anti-realist, constructivist accounts (appealing at this point to Devitt's arguments), and then suggests as the most plausible hypothesis to account for this objectivity (left unexplained by Devitt) the creative mind and will of God, who makes and sustains the objective world as what it is, irrespective of our human minds – but also including our human minds when they appear upon the scene. I stress the point that in addition to explaining objectivity and truth, this hypothesis explains the capacity of the world to evolve minds capable of discovering and affirming truth (the physicalist conception of which was an implausible feature of Devitt's position). J. R. Searle, in his Reith Lectures, *Minds, Brains and Science*[6] confessed to his inability to reconcile the scientific pressure for explanation in terms of 'bottom-up' (i.e. purely physicalist) causality with our manifest mental experience of 'top-down' causality. Theism resolves this impasse by subordinating material 'bottom-up' causation to divine 'top-down' causation, which at the same time accounts for there being instances of 'top-down' causation in those products of creation intended to bear and manifest the 'image of God'.

The argument from objectivity and truth to God is reinforced by recognition of the way in which abandonment of belief in an objective God has as a matter of historical fact spawned that whole host of anti-realist, constructivist views; whose implausibility may be apparent to common sense and science, but which common sense and science find it hard to rebut without appeal to God.

In a nutshell, the argument from truth to God is this: our deep-rooted conviction that truth is a matter of discovery and not invention is best accounted for – especially in its fullest scope, that is to say, including the truths of mind as well as of matter – on the supposition of an infinite creative Mind that makes things what they are and preserves them as what they are for us to discover.

So far, I have written rather simplistically of reality and truth as a question of things being what they are and their being known or believed to be what in fact they are. Of course, the theistic hypothesis does rather more than account for things being what they are. Certainly, if God made the world, then things are what they are because he so ordains. But the world does not only consist of its basic stuff, its fundamental constants, the laws of nature and the natural kinds that have evolved. As this last factor – evolved natural kinds – indicates, the world is in process and, on the theistic hypothesis, the divine mind ordains not only what there is, but what there will be and what there ought to be. Our discovery of truth includes our discovery of value and of the purpose and destiny of the world and of life.

I referred in the previous chapter to axiological arguments for the existence of God, suggesting that the objectivity of value is best explained by reference to an absolute ground of value. Another way of looking at the present argument is to see it as extending axiology to include the objective value of truth. The objectivity of things, like the objectivity of goodness and beauty, is best explained by the postulation of an absolute ground.

The postulation of God's creative will enables us to account not only for the objectivity of things (and of values) but also for two other facts in our experience. One has been mentioned already – the very fact that the universe includes minds that can come to believe and know the truth. The other is the fact that the world is knowable. The intelligibility of things is also a pointer to the mind of the Maker. This goes for the knowability of all natural kinds, and of what they are composed of, and of the basic laws of nature. We discover the world to consist of intelligible things and to constitute an intelligible system. The story of modern science greatly increases our conviction of and our wonder at the rationality of God's creation. Indeed, it is the rationality and intelligibility of what we find that encourages us to think of it as God's creation. It is interesting to note that this fact has thrust its apologetic force upon that otherwise redoubtable Barthian, T. F. Torrance, whose theology was briefly discussed in chapter four.[7]

I am not suggesting that we discover there to be only one fundamental and all-encompassing truth. The world consists of many things and we discover many truths. The idealist supposition that particular truths are somehow relative or incomplete and that only the one Absolute deserves the name of truth without qualification is as repugnant to common sense and to science as are the anti-realist constructivist theories mentioned above. But we do discover the connectedness of things in an intelligible universe; and the supposition of a single mind and will behind the one system and its many products justifies to some extent Anselm's view expressed in *De Veritate* that in discerning the truth of how particular things are, we gain some points of access to the supreme truth of God.

Given that the starting point of the argument from truth to God is the fact that we do discover how things are in the world prior to and irrespective of our minds and interests, something more must perhaps be said to counter the main sceptical argument against this premise – the argument that turned Putnam into a renegade – namely the argument that there is no way in which we can get outside our conceptual or linguistic skin and compare the way we see and talk about the world with how the world is in itself. Once again we have to take our stand here on common sense and insist that this sceptical argument is a very perverse argument. As was argued above,[8] our senses and our understanding should not to be thought of as a kind of screen cutting us off from the real world. They are the evolved and learned means of our perception of and thought about the real world. Admittedly, our senses and the common concepts in terms of which we classify and use things do not give us the whole story. But far and away the most plausible hypothesis to account for the way in which we have learned to see the natural world is that that is how it actually is. This hypothesis is then confirmed by scientific investigation into the further properties and basic structure of things, both observable and unobservable. The very idea of our trying or wanting to get outside our senses and concepts in order to see how accurately they portray the real world is quite absurd, if our senses and concepts are themselves our means of direct access to the world. The metaphor of portrayal or representation in any case begs the question. We do not perceive a portrait or even an image of a sheep when we look at a sheep. We have learned to apply the concept of a sheep to the object there before us in the field – and I do not mean in our visual field. That too is a metaphor and a phenomenalist abstraction prescinding from the actual relation in which we stand to the objects out there.

All this is quite clear to physicalist realists such as Devitt, though their account of the relation between a perceiver and a sheep will suffer from their determination to give a purely physicalist account of that relation. Much more plausible is an account which does full justice to the mental states and acts involved in seeing, identifying and thinking about the sheep in the field. This means that we have to reckon with an objective world containing not only stars and planets, fields and sheep, but thinking and knowing beings too.

On this basis we proceed to look for an explanation of there being an objective, stable world containing both things and persons, of its manifest knowability, and of our ability to come to know it in the way we do. The argument of this chapter has been that much the most plausible explanation of all these facts is that both the world and human beings are creatures with a God-given and God-preserved nature. And when we observe how fragile is the human hold on reality – the reality of things as well as of persons and values – once theism is jettisoned by our allegedly enlightened moderns, our conviction of the necessity as well as the plausibility of the theistic hypothesis is strengthened. The post-Nietzschean decline into a philosophy, as well as an art and theatre, of the absurd yields the supreme example of a *reductio ad absurdum* argument; and this supports the argument from manifest truth and objectivity to God as the creator and guarantor of that truth and objectivity.

8

Religions – theistic and non-theistic

One of the major developments in Christian theology in the modern world has been brought about by our increasing knowledge of and contact with other religions. Acquaintance with the scriptures and traditions of other faiths and, even more, acquaintance with the faith and spirituality of men and women of other faiths, have made it increasingly difficult for Christians, including Christian theologians, to assert, without qualms, the exclusive claims of Christianity or its status as the culmination of the history of religions. It is not easy to maintain even the finality of Christ in the context of a plurality of developed world religions. One of the effects of the phenomenological study of the religions of mankind (that is, the uncommitted, objective, though empathetic study of religion) has undoubtedly been to increase the pressure towards a relativistic understanding of religion and the religions.

The Second Vatican Council reflected something of these rational and moral pressures in its positive evaluation of the ethics, spirituality and theism of many great world faiths, although, understandably and perhaps rightly, it did not question traditional Christian belief in the finality of Christ.[1] At the end of this chapter we shall consider how it might be possible to hold on to the finality of Christ and at the same time to give due recognition to the religious worth of other faiths.

But the main issue to be tackled here stems not so much from the challenge to uniqueness and finality which Christianity must face in the light of the phenomenology of religion, but rather from the even more radical suggestion that religious pluralism is indicative of the non-cognitive, or non-fact-asserting status of religious faith. The sheer variety and, for each religion's participants, the life-enhancing quality of all the great world faiths – and, for that matter, of tribal religions too in many respects – can reinforce the suspicion that religion as such is not, after all, a matter of the long search for God, still less of responses to divine revelation, but rather a whole variety of socially constructed ways of coming to terms with life and of living ethically and spiritually fruitful lives both individually and in community. This, of course, is the voluntarist, expressivist, non-dogmatic understanding of religion which is under scrutiny in this book. The comparative study of religion, it is suggested, only serves to reinforce this view; for Christianity appears, to the student of religion, to be no more than one of the many possibilities in the spectrum of human religious ideals.

Sociology of religion, too, can reinforce the idea that religion functions as a system of ideas and practices that *make* the world a meaningful and bearable place for human beings to inhabit. Thus Peter Berger, applying to religious belief the techniques of the sociology of knowledge, writes that 'religion is the audacious attempt to conceive of the entire universe as being humanly significant'.[2] This, in itself, is an ambiguous statement. It could be taken to mean that such a daring conception is possible and actual just because in such a context of belief and practice the world is *found* to be an ultimately meaningful place. But it could also, and perhaps more naturally, be taken in a purely constructivist sense as meaning that in the religions, man constructs ways of thinking of the world and acting in the world (reinforcing them with rituals and spiritual exercises) which transform a meaningless material existence into a humanly meaningful life–world.

Reflection on the variety of forms of the religious life, both diachronically through history and synchronically across the world today, raises the well-worn topic of the *definition* of religion. What is it that identifies a phenomenon as a religion or as a specifically religious form of life? This question can be approached phenomenologically, bracketing issues of ultimate truth and reality, or it can be approached philo-sophically or theologically. Even from a phenomenological perspective, two radically different answers can be given, depending on whether one looks primarily at the alleged *object* of religious consciousness or at the characteristic subjective *attitudes* involved in religious forms of life. The former would lead to a definition in terms of man's alleged perception of and response to transcendence – to an alleged power or powers behind or beyond the world around us, which are believed to rescue man from his predicament, enable spirituality and ethical commitment, and sustain man's life beyond death into an eternal destiny. The latter approach, concentrating on subjective attitudes, would locate the essence of religion in feelings of ultimate concern, uncon-ditional disinterestedness, idealistic – perhaps ideological – commitments to overarching schemes of value. It is this latter kind of definition, in terms of the subjectivity of committed people, that enables secular ideologies such as communism to be classified as religions. (Paul Tillich, rather more sensibly, called them 'quasi-religions'.[3])

Cupitt's position, interestingly, conflates these two approaches to the definition of religion. For the alleged religious object – transcendence, the Absolute, God – is itself regarded by him as a projection or personification of the values and ideals to which believers are committed. In a sense, all religions, on an expressivist view, are assimilated to Tillich's quasi-religions. Only in some of them, however, are

116

men's ultimate concerns symbolised by or reified into a transcendent God-figure.

One world religion stands out by its explicit refusal to become involved in metaphysical claims about ultimate reality or God. Early Buddhism is not the only non-theistic religion in history, but it is peculiarly attractive to religious minds of a non-dogmatic, anti-metaphysical persuasion just because it concentrates so purely and exclusively on the way to liberation, rather than on speculation about the ultimate. Cupitt's predilection for early Buddhism and his self-appellation as a 'Christian Buddhist' clearly reveal his own non-theistic preferences, notwithstanding lip-service paid to the religious worth of 'God' as a symbol for our highest value and ideal.

But one should ponder the nature, limitations and fate of the religion of the Buddha rather more carefully before conceding it a paradigmatic status for religion in the modern world. For one thing, the non-theistic nature of Theravada Buddhism has been questioned. This is not so much a matter of doing justice to the residual place of 'the gods' in the Buddha's teaching. It is rather a matter of sensing, behind the Buddha's teaching on release into nirvana an inarticulate recognition of a transcendent state, admittedly impersonal and incapable of positive characterisation, that contradicts naturalism and empiricism just as sharply as does theistic metaphysics. Moreover, it is this feature of early Buddhism that reinforces our willingness to speak of it as a religion rather than as simply an ethic or a quasi-religion in Tillich's sense. To appreciate this point, we do not have to go as far as theologians such as John Hick, who at one time interpreted the Buddha's teaching on nirvana as itself reflecting an inarticulate awareness of an aspect of the transcendent *God*.[4] But it is interesting to note the possibility of such an interpretation.

The experienced limitations of Theravada Buddhism in the

history of religion are perhaps more important to observe for our purposes here. The austere, anti-metaphysical concentration on the way to overcome the craving behind all suffering, characteristic of early Buddhism, did not, as a matter of historical fact, succeed in meeting the religious needs of the people. This is one of the reasons for the striking revival of Hinduism, to the virtual exclusion of Buddhism, in India itself. But it is also reflected in the development of Mahayana Buddhism in the Far East. The newer emphases on the eternal Buddha nature, on the spiritual resources of the celestial Buddhas for their devotees on earth, and on the hopes for a more positive peace and enlightenment beyond death, are indicative of religious needs that were not being met by the earlier forms of Buddhism. That these religious needs are not to be understood in psychological terms alone, but rather as further cognitive intimations of the transcendent, is suggested by the metaphysical considerations which we have examined in chapters six and seven, and which most other religions have found themselves unable to ignore.

So, while it is quite clear that the Buddha constitutes an attractive figure for religious people of a sceptical anti-metaphysical cast of mind, there remains in Theravada Buddhism a narrowing down both of religious experience and interest and of philosophical concern that make it a poor key for understanding the history of religions and a less than adequate paradigm for religion today. This judgement is partly based on historical, phenomenological grounds, partly on religious, theological grounds, and partly on philosophical, metaphysical grounds. Phenomenologically speaking, we have observed that Theravada Buddhism neglects many elements usually thought important, even central, in religion. Religiously speaking, we have observed that it failed to satisfy the religious needs of people in India. Philosophically speaking, we have observed that it ignores the metaphysical difficulties of scepticism and naturalism and the metaphysical arguments for theism. Precisely the same observations are to be made of Cupitt's expressivist and voluntarist interpretation of Christianity.

Before we turn to look for a more adequate definition and interpretation of religion, it is worth pausing to ask why Cupitt himself prefers Christianity to Buddhism. After all, the two religions' moral and spiritual ideals of disinterestedness and inner discipline are strikingly similar, and Buddhism lacks the theistic metaphysics which, in Christianity's case, requires the most drastic demythologisation to make it fit Cupitt's view. There seems to be no reason for this preference. It can only rest on the historical contingency that Cupitt is a Westerner, nourished in the Christian tradition.

Phenomenological considerations not only lead us to question the paradigmatic status of Buddhism in the history of religions, but also to prefer a definition of religion in terms of its alleged object rather than in terms of attitudes alone. On such a phenomenologically based definition, religion consists in a set of attitudes, practices, institutions and beliefs evoked by and appropriate to some alleged transcendent source and goal of the world and of life.

We shall now proceed to consider a number of philosophical and theological interpretations of religion, thus defined.

Perhaps the best known is that of Rudolf Otto, whose basically Kantian extension of the a priori to include the irreducible dimension of the numinous and the holy was mentioned in chapter five.[5] Otto's approach was phenomenological in that he showed, with a wealth of illustration from the history of religions, the pervasive presence in human life of an entirely *sui generis* sense of awesome, yet fascinating mystery. But Otto went beyond phenomenology in assessing this numinous experience as experience *of* some numinous object, often thought of as a holy, demanding presence and power. Otto was not simply noting the frequency of such an interpretation of numinous experience. His was a philosophical, even theological judgement on the basic validity of the phenomenon in question. Sympathetic scrutiny of the world of religion not only uncovers this unique experience, it evokes it, and carries within itself conviction of its cognitive force. We find ourselves confronted by the holy.

Another, somewhat different example of phenomenology passing into philosophy is to be found in the work of Mircea Eliade. Eliade defined religious myths as 'the true dreams of mankind'.[6] The influence of Jung[7] is to be discerned behind this definition. But Eliade saw the truth of life coming to expression not so much in the 'unconscious' as in the myths and doctrines of religion – that is to say in public rather than private articulations of meaning. Moreover, Eliade is more explicit than Jung about the cognitive force of man's religious experience. Religions are not just *existentially* meaningful phenomena. They provide for men and women ways of more or less appropriate orientation on the real. And, as with Jung's archetypes, recurring features – common patterns – in world religion, indicate comparable modes of access to the same underlying meaning and reality. Interestingly, Eliade thought that the archaic religions and the eastern religions provided a deeper mode of orientation on the real than do the religions of Semitic origin (Judaism, Christianity and Islam) with their linear goal-directed views of history. All the same, we cannot ignore the ontological implications of Eliade's understanding of the significance of religion. For Eliade, reality as such has a spiritual rather than a material structure at bottom.

Turning to a more specifically theological figure, we may note the views of the great German sociologist of religion, Ernst Troeltsch. Troeltsch moved in an increasingly relativist direction, giving up his earlier attempts to rank the major world religions in an order of lesser or greater 'absoluteness'; but even from his later relativist viewpoint, Troeltsch saw the religions of mankind as mediating, in their various and complementary ways, genuine encounters with 'the Divine Spirit ever pressing the finite mind onward towards further light and fuller consciousness, a Spirit Which indwells the finite spirit, and Whose ultimate union with it is the purpose of the whole many-sided process'.[8] It is interesting to observe that what drove Troeltsch in an increasingly relativist direction was detailed sociological study of the empirical phenomena of religious history and life. But my present point is simply that such empirical study can still be suggestive of interpretation in terms of different culturally shaped responses to the pressures of transcendence, that is, of an objective divine Spirit, and precisely not a series of purely human projections.

A similar way of regarding the history of religions is currently being developed by John Hick, whose defence of theism solely by appeal to religious experience was mentioned in chapter four. Hick prefers the term 'pluralism' to 'relativism', and has for some years been urging a Copernican revolution in the theology of religion, whereby Christian theology is to forsake its Christocentrism and recognise that Christianity is but one channel in the history of God's saving encounters with mankind. Hick has gone to great lengths in trying to show how all the religions of the world, despite their surface differences, constitute points of contact with a spiritual ultimate, variously called 'God', 'the Eternal One', 'ultimate reality', 'the transcendent', 'the Real'.[9] It is important to note how the logic of his argument has driven him increasingly to prefer the vaguer, more neutral term 'the Real' to the theistic term 'God', in order to accommodate the non-theistic as well as the theistic religions in his picture of the universe of faiths. Nevertheless, Hick's understanding of religion, in all its diverse manifestations, remains cognitive, in the sense that all the major religions are seen as vehicles of liberating experience of the transcendent source and goal of the world and human life.

I have drawn attention to the work of Otto, Eliade, Troeltsch and Hick in order to show how serious study of the history and phenomenology of religion does not necessarily lead us in the direction of purely constructivist or projectional theories of religion. The argument from religion for the existence of God is not overthrown by consideration of the variety of religious experience. On the contrary, as the work of these scholars suggests, the history of religions is itself indicative of transcendence – of the reality of an ultimate source of being and value, which is, however partially and approximately, perceived by man's religious sense. If we allow ourselves, as Hick regrettably does not, to supplement the appeal to religious experience by the metaphysical and axiological arguments outlined in chapters six and seven, we may well suppose that such a cognitive account of the phenomenon of religion is much the most plausible account, all things considered.

There is, however, something of a warning signal in the way in which Hick's understanding of religion and the religions has developed. I pointed out how Hick's character-isation of the transcendent object of all religious experience is becoming more and more vague and empty of content, as he struggles to accommodate the diverse plurality of the religions of the world within a single global perspective. Ironically, the arch-defender of a cognitive theory of religion is moving towards a position scarcely to be differentiated from non-cognitivism; and it is hardly surprising to find non-cognitivists such as Cupitt increasingly claiming him as an unwitting ally.

The reason for this tendency in Hick's recent thought has nothing to do with the experiential basis of theism, which he still, to a considerable extent, shares with Otto, Eliade and Troeltsch. It is rather a consequence of his refusal – for fear of having to 'grade' religions – to countenance any important or ultimate differentiation in the actual content of religious experience as mediated by the various theistic and non-theistic religions, still less to supplement appeal to experience by appeal to both reason and revelation in the manner defended in chapter six.

It is appropriate at this point to turn again to the writings of Wolfhart Pannenberg, whose rational defence of Christian theism was mentioned in chapter four.[10] Pannenberg is certainly not opposed to general anthropological arguments designed to bring out the fact of man's universal openness to the transcendent; but, in an important article,[11] he argues (in fact against Troeltsch, though the point could equally be made against Hick) that on such a pluralist or relativist view the very possibility of a normative or decisive revelation from beyond is ruled out from the start. Close scrutiny of the history of religions, however, demonstrates not only that such claims to normative revelation are made, but that universality and finality are of the essence of the traditions of faith in question. This is true not only of Christianity, but of Islam and Hinduism (despite its syncretistic inclinations) and even of Buddhism in its categorical denial of metaphysical and theistic concerns. The historical religions themselves strongly resist accommodation within a Copernican global theology. There is no avoiding, then, in inter-faith dialogue, the exploration of mutually incompatible, normative beliefs, and assessment of them for their rational, moral and religious power to make the most sense of the world and of life and of history, including the whole history of religions.

In the course of this exploration, discriminations must be made and preferences stated. In the first place those religions which involve the affirmation of personal theism, most notably Judaism, Christianity, Islam, devotional Hinduism, Sikhism and much tribal religion as well, will concur in deeming to be religiously (and metaphysically) inadequate all the non-theistic religions and philosophies of the world, notwithstanding their ethical (and, in a sense, spiritual) depth and excellence. The religions of Semitic origin, for example, hold that the ultimate source of all being and value has explicitly revealed himself as personal and not impersonal. It is of the essence of these faiths, not only to reject impersonal monism and non-theistic agnosticism, but to resist relegation to the status of a partial, one-sided apprehension of something that transcends the personal or combines the personal and the impersonal.

Within the theistic faiths, further discriminations have to be made, and, in the dialogue of religions, representatives of each will expound and defend their own special view of the path to knowledge of God and of what that knowledge consists in. It is, of course, incumbent upon all the partners in a dialogue situation to discover and affirm what they have in common. They must indeed press beyond superficial dissimilarities to the deep mutualities of faith and spirituality that characterise the theistic religions of the world. But it is also incumbent upon the representatives of each normative faith to give reasons why their own traditions have affirmed a final revelation and claimed that, within the history of religions, a decisive event or word or incarnation has occurred. It is in this connection that we encounter Christianity's characteristic affirmation that God has finally revealed himself, his nature and his will, as well as what it is to be a human being and what is the destiny of man, in the Incarnation of his Word or Son in Jesus of Nazareth.[12]

Each faith, today, has to make sense of a world of different faiths. Theology of religions is high on the agenda, not only of the philosophy of religion, but also of each faith's own theological self-understanding. Christianity's incarnational Christology, its conviction of the uniqueness and finality of Christ as God the Son made man for the salvation of the world, stands out starkly in the history of religions as something impossible to reduce or relativise to one among many equally valid channels of divine–human encounter.

Moreover, it is precisely reflection on the particularity and claimed normativeness of Christian incarnational doctrine that may lead us to propose a more satisfactory Christian global theology of the religions than the pluralist solution advocated by Hick. We do not have to disparage the faith and spirituality of other traditions in order to recognise that a genuine incarnation, revelatory of God's essence and his very self in an actual human life, goes beyond any other kind of divine self-manifestation, and can, in the nature of the case, only happen once. Of course, God does not leave himself without witness elsewhere in human history, and much of great moral and spiritual worth is to be found in other faiths. But the one particular incarnate life of God is bound to be a revelation of surpassing value, normative in relation to all else, and universal in its significance.

Its universality makes it all-inclusive rather than exclusive. If Christ is indeed the incarnation of that 'person' in God, through whom the world was made, it must in reality be none other than the Spirit of Christ that vivifies and sustains morality and spirituality wherever they are to be found. The Christian, therefore, will expect to find marks of that Spirit in the faith of other men. He will also expect all men everywhere, in the end, to be drawn within the saving scope of Christ's life, death and resurrection. If this involves postulating further phases of the creative process beyond death in which those who have not had the chance to make their response to Christ as the 'human face of God' – and, one hopes, those too who have rejected him – may be drawn within the sphere of Christ's transforming influence, then so be it.[13] This eschatological resolution of the problem of Christianity and other faiths is surely to be preferred to a pluralistic reduction which evaporates the specific content not only of Christianity but of the other faiths as well. It is also to be preferred to a non-cognitivist reduction, which, by treating all religions as merely human, this-worldly constructions, necessarily entails the categorical rejection of belief in life after death.

9
Life after death

The conviction that belief in life after death is superstition presupposes a purely naturalistic world view. We may agree that independent philosophical arguments for immortality, such as those put forward by Plato and Descartes, carry little, if any, weight. But equally, arguments against immortality will only convince and seem obviously true and valid if a theistic framework of interpretation is excluded from the start. As we shall see, a number of purely anthropological considerations may be suggestive of immortality; but certainly they all fall far short of proof. And, in any case, they are perhaps more plausibly construed as suggestive of a whole theistic view of the world in which belief in life after death is embedded as an intelligible, even necessary, element. My present point is simply that where life after death is written off as quite impossible and belief in life after death derided as superstition we may be sure that a naturalistic – not necessarily materialistic, though usually science-based – conception of man as no more than a complex product of nature is being assumed. And indeed, even where man's mental and cultural life is recognised as the extraordinary phenomenon that it is, the human mind's increasingly appreciated dependence on our nature as highly developed biological organisms makes it extremely difficult for the empirically inclined to envisage the survival of personality beyond the death and dissolution of its bodily base.

It is true that an increasing number of religious believers themselves profess agnosticism or even disbelief on the subject of life after death, but this too illustrates the contemporary invasion of religion by naturalism. On investigation, the religion of such sceptics is found to be precisely of that voluntarist, pragmatic kind that Cupitt brings to articulate expression. Indeed, this is his peculiar constituency – those whose religious attitudes and commitments have somehow survived the erosion of metaphysical belief and subscription to Christian doctrine.

I intend to argue in this chapter, by contrast, that belief in life after death is inextricably bound up with belief in God and indeed is the 'acid test', as Austin Farrer put it,[1] of a serious belief in God. Moreover, expectation of a future life beyond death is one of the chief ways in which the objectivity of God and the cognitive nature of belief in God are shown. This is the point of John Hick's use of the phrase 'eschatological verification'.[2] The difference made by theism to one's whole view of the world is shown among other things, but perhaps most clearly, by its entailments regarding life after death. The believer in God hopes for and expects the world story, including his own story, to go on, in a transformed mode, beyond his own death and indeed beyond the 'heat-death' of the universe. This concomitant expectation, therefore, both indicates the metaphysical nature of belief in God and finds its rational ground in that belief.

The main argument of this chapter will be 'from above'. Defence of belief in life after death will be predominantly a matter of showing how it is entailed by a serious theism. Of course, that deduction cannot be made in isolation. At the same time, one has to show how the whole world in which such an expectation finds its place looks from a theistic viewpoint. And that means making connections with the world of ordinary experience. A theistic reading of the world together with its eschatological implications has to be shown to possess some kind of 'empirical fit', to borrow a term from Ian Ramsey.[3] Consequently, it is not unreasonable to *begin* 'from below' with an indication of some of the empirical factors that indicate and match up with the theistic view, including its future hope. I must repeat that the factors now to be considered provide not only intimations of immortality but first and foremost intimations of God. The following section, therefore, to some extent reiterates some of the grounds for belief in God given in chapter six.

A striking feature of the work of many of the modern Protestant and Catholic theologians mentioned in chapter four is the way in which they begin with a general anthropology designed to refute naturalism and to show what it is about man that raises the question of transcendence. I too will begin with anthropological considerations.

Man's relatively recent discovery of his roots and place in nature has tended to prevent him from maintaining a balanced view of his unique capacities and qualities. Evolutionary theory, molecular biology, sociobiology, empirical psychology and information theory have combined to encourage a purely naturalistic view of man as a naked ape, a mechanism for preserving the gene pool, a product of social forces and inbuilt instincts, a complex cybernetic system sustaining individual and corporate life in ever more complex conditions. Many aspects of man as a product of nature have indeed been greatly illuminated by advances in the natural and the human sciences, but one has only to reflect on one's experience, from within, and through interpersonal relation, of rationality, freedom and personality, to become aware how man transcends his biological roots. Consciousness is hard enough to account for in purely scientific terms; but when we reach the level of self-consciousness, we enter an irreducible sphere of self-transcendence, openness and creativity, immediately suggestive of a wider meaning and purpose than can be accounted for in terms of the interaction of physical elements alone. In chapter six, I emphasised the argument for the existence of God that rests precisely on the fact that the fundamental substance of the universe manifestly has the power to evolve rational persons. Here I simply advert to the fact that reflection on the emergence of what Teilhard de Chardin called the 'noosphere'[4] yields intimations of a creative intention behind the world process, a wider meaning in the world process, and, correlatively, a future beyond physical death.

Four features of human existence may be cited as raising these questions and pointing in the direction of a transcendent goal as well as a transcendent source of the world process: rationality, morality, art and religion.

Attention has already been drawn to what has been called the 'fine tuning' of the universe, that is, the extreme specificity and narrowness of range of the initial conditions in the universe's very early history, which alone made organic life and finite rational personal being possible, perhaps inevitable, in the course of cosmic evolution. The point of the argument was the suggestion of design, of an intention, and thus of a mind and will behind the cosmic process. The fact that the universe has it in it to produce a Newton and an Einstein, capable of unravelling the secrets of nature, is at least suggestive of this cosmic teleology. It is equally suggestive of a goal to the whole process beyond what is already achieved. On a purely naturalistic view, of course, it makes no sense to think in terms of a higher mode of life, beyond the bounded span of our earthly existence; but once a purpose or intention behind the cosmic story is discerned, it becomes implausible to think of rationality and personality as the temporary outcome of a system designed to produce no more than a series of brief lives, that series itself being no more than a temporary phenomenon in the long history of cosmic evolution. Both the nature and the value of human life (and that of any other rational beings there may be), in the context of cosmic teleology, cry out for more in the way of a transcendent goal or consummation to the process than their often prematurely curtailed life-spans allow. Human beings, with their manifest self-transcendence and openness to the future, as even Nietzsche saw – though in a very different sense – seek or will eternity.[5] What from within the framework of naturalism seems vain wishful thinking, within the scope of cosmic teleology seems a rational hope. Equally, the value of human existence, the perceived worth of rationality and personality, once cosmic purpose is acknowledged, provides intimations of a lasting destiny for man. It is hard to believe that an intention to bring into being a world of rational agents or persons can be satisfied with the realisation of such great, but ephemeral value as the history of man on earth exhibits.

Already I have spoken of value; and it is especially the phenomenon of moral goodness in the world that provides a basis for the notion that moral values cannot simply be the ephemeral products of human desires and aversions. The sociologist, Peter Berger, saw in the recurrent fact of human, moral outrage at radical evil a 'signal of transcendence',[6] a factor unaccounted for in purely sociological terms. But the positive moral values too, especially that of altruistic love, far transcend the ability of sociobiology to explain in terms of survival mechanisms, whether for the species or for the gene. I have already urged that both moral goodness itself and the unconditional claims of morality upon us are indicative of an ultimate source of value, itself supremely valuable. But now I want to urge that, if goodness and love have a securer basis in the nature of things than their precarious foothold in our ordinary human experience might suggest, then here too we detect an intimation of immortality. A world order, designed to produce and reflect moral value would be incoherent if that derivative value were not sustained beyond the death of the individual. If the universe is intended to evolve moral beings, then the mind behind that intention could hardly rest content with the lives of the saints cut short. Once again a cosmic teleology, productive of love, points beyond itself to love's consummation.

Aesthetic considerations are also not irrelevant to this theme. Wordsworth, in his 'Ode: Intimations of Immortality from Recollections of Early Childhood' may have focussed, somewhat over-romantically, on recollections of childhood's delight in the beauty of the earth, but we may well share his sense that in aesthetic experience and especially in the contemplation of natural beauty 'our souls have sight of the immortal sea, Which brought us hither'. Now, while it would be absurd to argue that our fleeting glimpses of beauty are pointless unless immortalised, it is not unreasonable to take such experiences as clues to the meaning of the world process. If so, neither beauty nor we, its beholders, can coherently be thought of as merely temporary values, destined for extinction. Only a naturalism that already repudiates teleology requires that view.

Of all the products of the human world, religion itself contains the fullest intimations of immortality. They were, it is true, only gradually acquired. Without a developed theistic framework of belief, religious notions of survival tend to be extremely vague and unattractive, the very reverse of wish-fulfilment, as John Hick has pointed out.[7] Moreover, the value of each human person as an end in himself is not appreciated in early or undeveloped stages of the history of religions. But especially in the contexts of the theistic world religions, reflection on the nature of man as a child of God, together with the devotional or mystical experience fostered in the various religious traditions, has given rise to many forms of belief in an afterlife. It is as a religious animal that man most obviously transcends nature, in both his sense of God and his hope of heaven. This hope can be expressed with great naivety, as a projection of all too earth-bound aspirations and it can be accompanied by excessive fears of hell and damnation, difficult to reconcile with a seriously moral idea of God's love and power. But certainly, for the religions, the significance and worth of human life, indeed the glory of man, have been brought out and undergirded by the sense that rooted in the earth though he is, he is made for eternity.

The phenomena of rationality, morality, art and religion, all of them in a sense products of evolution, yet at the same time marks of nature's self-transcendence in the phenomenon of man, have always prompted philosophers of an idealist persuasion to think of mind or spirit as the ultimate category in terms of which alone an adequate account of reality can be given. Nature itself, on such a view, can only be understood on the basis of what has emerged from it. Mind, and all the spiritual values associated with the world of mind, provide the best clues for an interpretation of the significance and destiny of the whole. But philosophical idealism suffers from two major drawbacks. It has tended to fight shy of drawing the full theistic consequences of postulating mind as the heart and source of all there is. And it has tended to undervalue the human person as an irreducibly valuable end in himself. The mind of man, whether that of the individual or more usually that of the group – chiefly the State – has been portrayed as but a temporary, albeit the highest, self-manifestation or expression of the Absolute in history. And the latter – the Absolute – although conceived on the analogy of mind or spirit – has not been consistently thought through in fully theistic terms. Only some of the so-called 'personal Idealists' have done justice both to the reality of God and to the significance and eternal destiny of each human person.[8]

I shall not pursue these matters any further 'from below', from the perspective of the kind of philosophical anthropology which culminates in Idealism. It is enough to have drawn attention to some of the intimations of immortality which constitute points of connection for the doctrines of a future state that we find to be taught in the developed, theistic, world religions. The fact that these intimations of immortality are already bound up with intimations of theism shows in any case that we cannot seriously attempt to defend belief in life after death apart from belief in God.

Since this book is concerned to refute a reductionist understanding of *Christianity*, the theological argument for immortality or resurrection will be restricted here to the Judaeo-Christian context. Parallel arguments could be examined in the contexts, among others, of Islam, devotional Hinduism, Mahayana Buddhism, Sikhism, and the religion of the Parsees, and much interesting comparative work undertaken along the lines suggested in chapter eight. But our present task is a more limited one: it is to demonstrate the implausibility of any attempt to demythologise *Christian* belief in life after death.

The basic structure of the argument is this: insofar as the Christian religion entails and requires belief in the reality of God (in the fully objective sense defended in previous chapters of this book), it follows from the revealed nature of God that he must and will raise the dead. This necessity, of course, is not imposed on God from anywhere else but his own nature as perfect goodness and love.

It took time, in the history of Israel's religion, for this implication of belief in God to be drawn out. It is there in the later prophets and in the apocalyptic writings of both the Hebrew Bible and the intertestamental period. As already pointed out, deeper appreciation of the character of God went hand in hand with greater appreciation of the value of the individual. Hammered out in the hard experience of national and personal disaster, these insights led to the conviction that 'the souls of the righteous are in the hand of God'[9] and that

God will raise his children, judge them and vindicate them in the last day. The matter was still disputed at the time of Jesus; but Jesus himself clearly sided with the Pharisees against the Sadducees in declaring that God is 'not God of the dead but of the living',[10] and in promising that all who believe in him will be raised by God at the last day.

The resurrection of Jesus from the dead, however we understand that mysterious event which brought about the birth of the Christian Church, was soon being interpreted as the decisive and revelatory anticipation of the eventual destiny of all God's children. Its significance was already manifest in the experience of the early Christians (whether in prayer or worship) of the risen Christ as a living Lord. It would have been inconceivable that a religion founded on the resurrection and sustained by the real presence of the risen Christ, could abandon its future hope for all.

These two factors – Christ's endorsement of the hope of resurrection and his own resurrection from the dead – led inexorably to the inclusion of the eschatological clauses in the early Christian creeds. Indeed it can reasonably be claimed that the themes of resurrection, judgement, and everlasting life have been just as central and determinative for Christian identity as have the doctrines of the Incarnation and the Trinity.

For Christianity is undoubtedly one of the major world religions that have encouraged us to think of the whole world process in linear historical terms as moving in a particular direction towards an intended transcendent goal or destiny. This is why evolutionary theory is in principle at home in Christianity and not opposed to it. But unlike naturalistic evolutionary theory, Christianity, with its conviction of the reality of God lying behind, within and ahead of all world history, is able to posit an ultimate fulfilment rather than an eventual petering out of the evolutionary, historical process.

Marxism too encourages us to think in linear historical

terms. As a child of the Judaeo-Christian tradition, it has inherited this fundamental stance that differentiates western civilisation from those oriental cultures which see the cosmos in static or cyclical terms. But Marxism, with its exaggerated antipathy to religion, has lost the capacity to speak of anything but an inevitably temporary climax to the historical process – a classless society, which, even if ever realised (and that seems increasingly unlikely, given the experienced nature of man and of power), will certainly not survive the 'heat-death' of the universe. Moreover, Marxism has no solution to the problem of the death, including the premature death, of individuals. Men and women can only struggle for a temporary, perhaps mythical goal, in which they themselves will never participate.

Christianity, by contrast, speaks of a trascendent consummation to the whole world process, in which all God's children, from every generation, will themselves participate. For God will raise the dead. I have endeavoured to resolve some of the problematic aspects of this area of Christian doctrine in my book, *The Christian Hope*.[11] Here I dwell simply on the fact that Christian hope of heaven rests wholly on the twofold foundation of the objective reality and the revealed character of God.

Belief in life after death is natural, intelligible and inevitable, if one is seriously a theist and at the same time holds that it has been revealed that God is love. Recognition that love made the world greatly enhances our ability to see the necessary connection between belief in God and belief in life after death. It was argued above that to discern an intention behind the world process is already to acquire intimations of immortality; for it is implausible to suppose that the production of life as we know it is by itself a sufficient justification for creation. To discern *love* behind the world process leads to a much stronger form of the same argument. The world as we know it, shot through though it is with astonishing beauty and moral value, is too costly a process in suffering and evil, with countless lives prematurely cut short and countless others lived in appalling circumstances. Whatever may be done, from Christian love or from whatever other motive, towards the amelioration of these conditions, the sheer accumulated weight of undeserved suffering strongly belies the claim that the world is the creation of a God of love – unless in fact God raises the dead and all along has intended to raise the dead.

There are many other things to be said in working out a Christian theodicy – in trying, that is, to answer the question why God permits so much suffering and evil in the world.[12] As already indicated, the process of cosmic evolution has to be seen as necessary to the formation of finite personal creatures, and the risk of suffering inextricably bound up with the formative process by which alone we can be made. Of course, it is the peculiar belief of Christianity that God accepts responsibility for the world's inevitable suffering and evil by taking it upon *himself* through the Incarnation and Cross. God's own costly, self-sacrificial love is enacted and manifested in the Cross, whereby men and women are drawn into close relation with their Maker and enabled to overcome the worst the world can do. But that overcoming is only a serious possibility both for God and for mankind, if resurrection did, does and will take place. Only if God raised Christ from the dead, bestowing the power of his risen life on all who are drawn to God through him, and in the end raising them too to the life of the world to come, can we seriously believe that the love of God manifested in the Cross in fact has the last word. And only so can such a costly creative process be morally justified. However successfully the theodicist spells out the necessities involved in the arduous creative process, during its formative phase, the creation will not seem worth the cost unless God brings about the intended consummation of that process and enables his personal creatures to share in that consummation.

Christian belief in life after death is primarily, therefore, a theological derivation from the revealed character of the God who made the world. Abandonment of this belief is a sign of a more basic abandonment of belief in God and in the love of God.

It will be clear that these implications of Christian theism are better spelled out in terms of resurrection than of immortality. Christianity does not teach a natural immortality, discernible by human reason alone. We are talking, rather, of a further phase in the creative process, a *new* creation, which transforms the present conditions of life into an incorruptible and permanent mode. All this can only be brought about by new creative acts of God. On the other hand, there must be some continuity between the old and the new if it is indeed to be the persons fashioned through the earth who are *themselves* to inherit everlasting life. Christian theology has an interest, therefore, in noting the ways in which human beings already transcend their empirical, biological base, and enter the world of the spirit. The above reflections on the intimations of immortality already available in this phase of the creative process are not irrelevant to the theology of resurrection required by Christian theism.

It was suggested, at the end of the last chapter, that we may well have to postulate further *phases* in the creative process, beyond death, in which God's personal creatures from all times, places, cultures and religions are enabled to grow into the knowledge and love of the triune God, whose incarnate Son, now risen and ascended, remains the permanent focus of all God–man relations. It is to be hoped that all human beings will, in the end, be reconciled and drawn into communal relation with the God and Father of our Lord Jesus Christ. The only credible alternative, for Christian belief, is not a permanent state of alienation or hell – that makes no moral sense at all – but rather the awesome possibility of annihilation, where a person has rendered himself completely unresurrectable. One hopes and prays that such an ultimate loss will never actually occur.

Cupitt writes movingly in *The Sea of Faith* of the moral ambiguities involved in the use by pastors of Christian eschatological hope in their ministry to the dying.[13] There is indeed much danger of unreality, insincerity and insensitivity in this work. There is a time to speak and a time to be silent on such issues. Moreover if, as has been argued here, the hope of heaven is a derivation from faith in God, it is the latter rather than the former that must shape and control one's approach to the death of others (as indeed to one's own death). Those ministering to the dying will of course respect the degrees of faith or unbelief in those to whom they minister. Where appropriate, their words and prayers will help the dying to hold on to what they have seen, however faintly, of God's eternal love. There is much that can be done, just humanly speaking, by silent presence and gentle care, to ease the passing of another human being. But specifically *Christian* ministry is only impoverished if it does not spring from and allow itself to be informed by a deep faith in the love of God, who will not let his fragile creatures go for ever.

10

The Christian Church and objective theism

The chief topic of this book has been the reality of God. My concern has been to argue the case for belief in God in an objective sense, and at the same time to show how such belief belongs to the essence of Christianity. If this is so, it follows that the Church, the community through which the Christian faith is practised and taught, is, for all time, committed to belief in the objective reality of God.

In the final chapter of this book I want to examine this entailment. Is it true that the Christian Church stands or falls by its commitment, for all time, to the objective reality of God? Is it conceivable that a Christianity and a Church without dogma and without metaphysical belief might continue to exist as a merely human vehicle of a particular 'religious' form of life?

There are a number of issues at stake here. In the first place there is the question of sociological realism: is it plausible to suppose that Christianity as a world religion and the Church as an institution could survive without its dogma and without its metaphysics? In other words, is it realistic to envisage the whole Church coming to adopt a purely expressivist understanding of its own language and liturgy? In the second place, there is the question of definition: would a Church that cut loose from belief in the objective reality of God count as a Christian Church at all? In the third place, and of course most basic and important of all, is the question of truth: is the Church in fact a community of response to divine revelation?

The first, the sociological question may be rephrased as the question whether a purely expressivist interpretation has the capacity to sustain Christianity as a world religion. It must be admitted that there are religions in the world which rely much less on dogma and metaphysics than historical Christianity has done. We considered the case of Theravada Buddhism in chapter eight. But the historical and phenomenological point to which I drew attention there, namely Theravada Buddhism's failure to sustain its place in India and its development into much more metaphysical and devotional forms in the Far East, was also a sociological point about what factors can actually sustain a world religion through history. It might be suggested that specifically modern conditions – including the collapse of metaphysical systems and the prevalence of more sceptical, science-based philosophies of life – favour the more pared-down, non-dogmatic religions such as early Buddhism, if they favour any religion at all. That is a big 'if' for, despite the popularity of non-theistic forms of Buddhism, including Zen, among considerable numbers of individuals today, not least in the West, the fact remains that Buddhism is on the defensive. It has not succeeded in withstanding the onslaughts of Marxism in South East Asia, and seems even more vulnerable, as a large-scale social institution, to the inroads of secularisation than does Christianity in the West. So the prospects for a Buddhistic form of Christianity seem pretty bleak.

The sociological plausibility of non-theistic forms of Christianity does not seem very high. There is the obvious point that a total or even large-scale, conversion of the historic Churches to an expressivist self-understanding seems extremely unlikely to say the least. More interesting and more important is the point that, even sociologically speaking, what sustains theistic religions such as Christianity (and Islam) against secularisation, communism and persecution is the strong faith in God that is so deeply embedded in the

Christian (and Muslim) consciousness. It is hard to see that, if acknowledged as such, a merely human 'religious' ideal, however socially reinforced, could succeed in preserving Christianity, generation after generation, in the many different contexts where it has taken root.

For the driving force of the Christian religion is undoubtedly its conviction of a saving power from beyond. As pointed out in chapter one, it is in the minds of its adherents a religion of grace, a religion that lives by its faith that man, in his weakness and inability to find from his own resources the way to wholeness and love, is taken out of himself, forgiven and enabled to grow in love by the Spirit of God and of Christ crucified and risen. Christians see their spirituality and ethics as flowing, not from their own strength but from the lived and experienced relation between believers and their· Lord. The very point of Christian worship, in both its sacramental and its non-sacramental forms, is claimed to be the conscious, communal articulation and sustenance of that relation. It is hard to see how Christianity could survive loss of the conviction that this is so.

The question of definition is less important and less decisive than the sociological question. I have claimed, on historical and phenomenological grounds, that Christianity is, in essence, a theistic religion and that theism is therefore central to its definition. In theory, this could change. The Christian Church could, as a whole or by majority vote or however, decide that in future Christianity is to be defined in non-theistic terms. The word 'Christianity' would thenceforth be given a different range of meaning. But nothing hangs on stipulated definitions. What can be claimed, on sociological grounds, is that such a decision is highly unlikely, and that, if it were made, Christianity would probably die out.

The sociological point has to be expressed in terms of belief: it is *conviction* of God's reality and God's grace that sustains Christianity as a world religion. But religiously and theologically, the point has to be expressed otherwise. For the believer, it is God's grace alone that nourishes and sustains the Christian and the Church, and makes Christianity – where it is so – an expression of God's love for the world. So the basic question is neither a sociological question about the power of belief systems nor a question of definition but a question of truth. The Church claims to *be*, in essence, a community of response to God's revelatory gift of himself in love to the human world and an instrument of God's saving love here on earth.

The argument of this book has been designed to support this conviction and to demonstrate the truth of its most basic element – belief in the objective reality of God. It follows that, without an objective God, Christianity not only would but *ought* to collapse like a pack of cards. For there would be something ethically improper in an attempt by the Church to re-define its self-understanding in such a way as to dispense with the reality of God. It would be morally repugnant as well as ineffective to try to deck out a merely human ethic and a merely human spirituality in Christian language, suitable re-defined, and to pretend that that is what Christians have really meant all along.

This is in no way to suggest that the Church should ignore the intellectual critique that has been mounted against its basic doctrines since the time of the Enlightenment and simply presuppose the truth of God without argument. On the contrary it is incumbent upon Christians to listen to criticism, to wrestle with doubt, and to argue with unbelief. Christian apologetic has an important function in the Church, namely that of showing the rational tenability of theism and of Christian doctrine. That includes arguments for the existence of God. For it is not enough to spell out the *inner* rationality of Christian doctrine, *given* belief in God. The view that Christian talk of God can only be spelled out from within the horizon of a committed faith stance – the view known polemically as 'fideism' – and the view that revelation alone creates the conditions for meaningful talk of God – the view known polemically as 'revelational positivism' – have both proved vulnerable to collapse precisely because they refuse, albeit out of the purest theological motives, to engage in the apologetic task. Even the philosophical theology of Alvin Plantinga and Nicholas Wolterstorff,[1] notwithstanding its logical rigour, is vulnerable on this score. For, although belief in God may well be basic in many peoples' belief systems, in the sense that, simply as a matter of fact, it is not for them the result of rational argument, it still remains vulnerable if denied rational support. It is too contentious a belief in the modern post-Enlightenment world to be justified by appeal to testimony or experience alone. Testimony and experience are very important in religion. The testimony of the saints and of those whose lives have been changed by divine grace is indeed indicative of the reality of God. So is the experience of God which many people claim, in however faint or mysterious a form. But unless these essential elements in religion can find support from rational reflection on the existence and nature of the world and on the values that have emerged in the course of evolution and history, religious faith remains vulnerable to alternative explanation.

Rational apologetic, essential though it is to the Church's task in the modern world, does not mean the defence of the status quo where Christian doctrine is concerned. There is plenty of room, indeed there is need, for the development of doctrine in the light of man's ever-expanding scientific knowledge, and in the light of the whole history of philosophy and theology. Even the doctrine of God develops; and, as earlier chapters in this book will have indicated, theism is defended and expounded by modern theologians in very different ways from its classical exposition, say, in Augustine or Aquinas. It is perfectly appropriate to explore, as John

Macquarrie does,[2] the possibilities of 'panentheism' (the view – not to be confused with 'pantheism' – that God's reality contains within itself the world's derived reality) or of process metaphysics.[3] These developments reflect a very proper suspicion of the influence of Platonism on classical theism and a very proper concern to relate belief in God to contemporary, science-based philosophies of nature. But there is all the difference in the world between revisionary conceptions of theism and what are put forward as non-theistic conceptions of Christianity. The Church can tolerate, even welcome, the former in a way it cannot tolerate the latter; for the former maintain, while the latter deny, the Church's very *raison d'être*, namely, its function as a witness to and vehicle of a resource and a grace from beyond nature and beyond humanity.

Such an understanding of the Christian Church, as a body bearing witness to, guarding, and promoting *divine* truth, and itself focusing the creation's response in worship to its Creator, is of course maintained and handed down by human beings who, in their own thought and experience, have found it to be true. Throughout this book I have tried to show both the phenomenological exactitude of this description and the rational grounds for accepting its truth. Admittedly the Church embraces people in very varied stages of conviction and commitment. It welcomes any who are attracted by the figure of Jesus and the Christian way, even if they have as yet discovered for themselves only a fraction of the truth of Christian doctrine. But, notwithstanding many Christians' doubts and conscientious reservations over matters of doctrine, the Churches could not possibly permit these doubts to determine the nature of Christian faith. The creeds, the confessions, the liturgies, and also the bishops and teachers of the Church are inextricably bound to the truth of God and must represent and transmit the heart of the faith, not only those aspects of it which some moderns find most easily assimilable, such as Christian ethics or Christian sense of community.

The heart of the faith is Christian discernment of the reality of God as the ultimate source of all life and love both here and in eternity. There is an ocean of truth here, in objective theism, to be discovered by all who embark upon the ship of faith and are prepared to use all their faculties, including reason, to chart its course. No doubt there is always more, beyond the horizon, than what the theologians or the Church can presently articulate. But the horizons already opened up – the vision of self-sacrificial love at the heart of all things, the experience of joy in creation and peace in reconciliation, the promise of healing and liberation for all life's victims, the hope of a perfected new creation in which God's personal creatures will participate for ever – these things more than justify the decision to embark.

Above all, this venture of faith in the reality of God is a liberating experience. One of the weirdest aspects of the evident appeal of a non-theistic, expressive interpretation of Christianity to some people on the fringes of the Church is that this pale, diminished shadow of authentic Christian faith is itself experienced as liberating. It is a measure of the Church's failure to live by or convey the truth that makes us free[4] that an atheist version of Christianity can be found liberating.

So, to conclude this defence of objective theism, the chief elements of Christian belief in God and the reasons for holding them to be true will be summarised. The summary will also hint at fresh vistas, on or beyond the horizon of objective theism.

Christians believe and trust in God the Father who made the world. That is to say, they believe that the whole universe, themselves included, depends for its very existence upon the creative will and intention of the absolute and ultimate source and ground of all there is. Since they think of this absolute ground in terms of will and intention, they necessarily experience it as personal, not impersonal. Christians inherit a long tradition of such theistic interpretation, going back to Israel's faith, which experienced God as a holy will, demanding obedience and inspiring awe as well as accounting for there being a created world at all. That tradition, made universally accessible by the Christian Church, was developed and changed over the centuries in the light of what both Jews and Christians call divine revelation. This involved the filling out of the primary theistic insight through the analogy of a father's love for his children. Christians continue to use this language, speaking of the creator God as Father, largely out of respect for the long tradition in which they stand. And indeed it expresses very well the dependence relation between God's personal creatures and their Creator and the status of being loved and cared for and enabled to grow into maturity and friendship with the very source of their being. But, nothing hangs on the use of 'father' rather than 'mother'. It is the parental relation which provides the analogy. In fact, Christians have discovered that they can speak of elements of motherhood as well as fatherhood in God; although God himself, of course, transcends utterly any specifically male or female symbolism.

As Christians in the Church inherit and reflect on this theistic tradition of understanding the world and its meaning, they come to *experience* for themselves in prayer and worship the religious reality of which it speaks. They find too that it makes sense of their existence and that of the whole world. This making sense is in part a matter of the internal rationality and illuminating power of Christian theism, as spelled out in the many centuries of imaginative and creative Christian theology. But it is in part a matter of coming to see that there are good reasons for belief in a creator God. An absolute, infinite, self-existing mind alone explains the contingency and yet the intelligibility of the universe. A personal will or intention alone explains the kind of order which the universe possesses – its capacity to evolve finite minds and the fine tuning of its initial conditions, if ever that capacity was to be realised. A supremely good and beautiful ultimate reality behind all finite forms of existence alone explains the values we perceive on earth in such partial, temporary and fragile ways. This holy will and power at the source of things explains, too, man's religious sense, his openness to the transcendent, the fact that throughout history and all over the globe man prays and worships and enjoys experience of God. And of course the reality and activity of God constitute the best explanation of the traditions of faith based on special revelation. All these factors – testimony, experience, reason and revelation – combine to make Christian faith in God and Father, who made the world, a well-founded belief.

Christians also believe and trust in God's Son Jesus Christ, who redeemed mankind. This further, specifically Christian belief has not featured as a major, pivotal element in the present study. We have been concerned, rather, with the fundamental belief in God which forms the presupposition of any further belief that God makes himself most personally and intimately known by coming amongst us in person in incarnate form as the man, Jesus of Nazareth. There is no point in discussing the possibility of God's incarnation until one is clear about the reality of God, as were the Jews amongst whom Christ came. But there is no doubt that incarnational theism, with its conviction that the hidden God is revealed and made accessible through incarnation, so that the life and fate and resurrection of Jesus Christ release among us the limitless resources of God for healing and renewal and communion with the living God, is an extremely potent form of theistic faith, both morally and spiritually speaking.

Belief in Jesus, God incarnate, is the starting point of Christian trinitarian theism. It is only the starting point; for by itself, while certainly suggestive of relation in God – love given and love received within the deity – it does not take us further than towards a dipolar, binitarian conception of God as containing within himself two 'persons' or centres of awareness, action and love. Discernment of such internal differentiation and relation in the deity, however, is a big step in the history of theism.

The reasons why Christians think in incarnational terms again consist in a combination of rational, historical, and experiential factors. In the first place, there is a great increase in rational plausibility if the ultimate ground of being can be seen not only in personal but also in interpersonal terms; for there is an incompleteness about the model of an individual, as though in essence it made sense to think of a personal God as subsisting in isolation, in undifferentiated unity. Then, secondly, rational reflection on what is claimed by Christians to be revealed in history, namely, the nature, will and intention of God, embodied and enacted in Jesus and his story, requires a relational model in order to explain how the love of God for his incarnate Son, Jesus, and the love of Jesus for his heavenly Father can be held to mirror and body forth, within creation itself, the eternal love, given and received, within God, before ever the world was made. Then, thirdly, rational reflection on Christian experience of the risen Christ, in prayer and sacrament, requires the Christian mind to maintain an internally differentiated concept of God; for Christians believe that they have a living representative in God himself, through whom they are drawn into relation with the Father.

But there is more to specifically Christian theism than this. For Christians also believe and trust in the Holy Spirit who gives life to the people of God. The specifically Christian experience of inspiration by the Spirit reveals a second relational polarity in God: the Holy Spirit of God not only comes forth from the transcendent God to energise us immanently from within; he actually takes us up into a further internal divine self-address, interceding for us, as St Paul puts it, 'with sighs too deep for words'.[5] This too is believed to mirror the divine relations in God as he is in himself.

Once again, in addition to these experiential grounds, there are good reasons for what must now be thought of as a fully trinitarian concept of God. For, as Richard Swinburne has argued in an unpublished paper, no concept of God can satisfy us, rationally speaking, that does not contain within itself the notion not only of sharing but of co-operation in sharing. Only a trinitarian God fulfils the criteria of absolute self-sufficient personality. This rational consideration may be held to illuminate and confirm the conviction of Christians down the ages that the Christian life is enabled and sustained precisely by the gift of the Holy Spirit, individually in their hearts, and communally in the fellowship of the Church. This Christian trinitarian belief deepens and explicates the central facts of dependence on God and relation to God which, as was stressed in chapter one, make Christianity the thing it is.

I have mentioned, without developing, these further, trinitarian ramifications of Christian theism, for two reasons. Firstly, it is necessary to reject as wholly misconceived the attempts by some theologians, Catholic as well as Protestant,[6] to set Christian trinitarian belief in God against and apart from theism, as though belief in God, Father, Son and Holy Spirit, were not firmly and for ever rooted in Jewish monotheism. And secondly, a general defence of objective theism, such as has been given in this book, and which no serious monotheist could dispute, must not be thought to exhaust the resources of belief in God – and indeed the resources of God – that full participation in the Christian Church makes available to men and women of faith. For it is by its faith in God, Father, Son and Holy Spirit not just by its faith in an objective God, that the Christian Church will stand or fall.

The Church's ministry

Have ordained ministers of the Church a responsibility to teach the objective reality of God? No doubt the primary loyalty of every man and woman is to the truth, as he or she perceives it. But it is not unreasonable to hold that Christian ministers are people who have, among other things, perceived the truth of Christian doctrine and, from a sense of vocation, offered themselves as stewards of the mysteries of God. It is as such that the Church commissions them and invests them with authority to teach the faith, not on their own behalf, but on the Church's behalf, as its spokesmen and spokeswomen.

It is undeniable that there exist among theologians, among ministers, and even among bishops, strong disagreements over doctrine. This has always been the case, and is doubtless inevitable. The prevalence of such internal conflict, since New Testament times, over what makes Christianity the thing it is, has recently been drawn to our attention in a book by Stephen Sykes.[1] Its inevitability is partly due to the transcendence of the object of Christian belief, namely the reality, nature and will of God, over any finite, limited, human representation of them, and partly to the necessary interactions and developments of Christian doctrine in relation to new knowledge in other spheres, such as science and philosophy. Christianity is bound, therefore, to be preached and taught in many different ways and in many disputed ways. But these differences and conflicts take place

150

within a certain range. There must be what Wittgenstein called a 'family resemblance'[2] between the different versions of Christianity. Just as not anything and everything could count as a 'game', so there are some beliefs and practices which have to be deemed to lie beyond the range of accredited or licensed forms of Christian teaching. It may be very hard to demarcate the boundaries of this range, but some things lie well outside them, and atheism is surely one such.

The Christian Church commissions its ministers to testify to the objective reality of God and to transmit the Gospel of the Incarnation. The Church is bound therefore to require of its ministers sincere faith in God. It would be absurd for bishops to ordain atheists. And if an ordained minister loses his faith in God, it would seem appropriate for him, indeed incumbent upon him, to resign his orders.

It is much the best thing for the Church to rely on its ministers' integrity in this matter, rather than institute disciplinary procedures against them. Experience has shown that Church authorities almost invariably lapse from general standards of equity, let alone Christian standards of love, when they have instituted proceedings for heterodoxy against a priest or minister. Recent examples in the Roman Catholic Church and in the Presbyterian Church in America do not inspire confidence. One recalls Karl Barth's wise advice in the case of Rudolf Bultmann, that such errant theology is best answered, on the one hand, by theological criticism within the community of Christian scholars and, on the other, by the Church's continuing faithfulness to the Gospel of Jesus Christ.[3]

It has to be admitted that the theological bones of contention that have in fact prompted attempts to discipline priests and teachers in the aforementioned Churches have not concerned the basic question of belief in an objective God. They have concerned rather such questions as infallibility, the divinity of Christ, the uniqueness and finality of Christ, moral theology, the authority of bishops, and belief in life after death. The teaching by ordained theologians of atheistic interpretations of the Christian faith might well be thought to put this tolerant policy of forswearing disciplinary measures, while answering them theologically and refusing to let their views affect Church doctrine and liturgy, under some strain.

The situation brought about by contemporary advocacy of a purely expressivist understanding of Christian God-talk might be deemed less straightforward than the hypothetical case of a priest advocating atheism. The expressivist view, after all, is claimed to be an interpretation of God-talk, not a repudiation of it. We are encouraged to suppose that what has commonly, throughout Christian history, been taken as referential – that is, as referring to an objective God, Creator of the world – is in fact a way of expressing commitment to an overarching ideal of disinterested love, with no necessary connection to metaphysical theism. As we have seen, the case is argued with great passion and singleness of mind. It is presented in connection with a very telling historical account of the challenge to the Christian tradition posed by post-Enlightenment modernity. But, as shown in this book, the expressivist view *is* tantamount to atheism. As such, it is not a tenable way for the Church to respond to the challenge of modernity. For the reasons given here, it is to be rejected by the Church, not only because it misrepresents the nature of Christian belief in God, but first and foremost because it presupposes an atheistic world view that is found, on examination, to be false.

The rejoinder might also be made that a Christian scholar ought to try to see what is of positive value in his opponent's views. He ought to put them in the most favourable light in order fairly to engage with them. For instance, if expressivists deny that they are atheists and claim, rather, merely to be interpreting Christian God-talk, then their colleagues ought to accept this as honestly and fairly meant, and not force them into an atheist mould. On the other hand, it is precisely because one sees the force of the expressivist solution to the challenge of modernity that one appreciates its atheistic character, notwithstanding the lip-service paid to God-talk. Purely expressivist interpretations of Christian talk of God *are* atheistic, if words mean anything at all. Certainly a Christian teacher should feel the force of the cultural, historical, and philosophical arguments against Christian belief in God. It is important to engage with them seriously and in depth in all apologetic work. A defence of Christian theism (and of belief in life after death) is all the more powerful when the apologist has evidently put himself, imaginatively, in the shoes of his agnostic or atheist critics.

But the waters are more than somewhat muddied when the critics are themselves ordained ministers, offering a non-theistic translation of the key elements in Christian doctrine from within the Church's teaching body itself. Curiously, an overt attack on Christian belief from outside the Church can be accorded much more sympathetic treatment. For the arguments against belief in God and life after death *are* serious arguments and, as I say, are best answered by those who have felt their force. But when those arguments are not only fully accepted but virtually presupposed by expressivist theologians, themselves ordained ministers of the Church, it is much less easy to be sympathetic and conciliatory. In such a situation, it only confuses the issue if one tries to extract the things of positive worth – the ideal, the commitment, the disinterestedness – from the atheism into which supposed spokesmen of the Christian Church have slipped. For have they not forgotten their commission to bear witness to the things of God?

Notes

PREFACE

1 D. Cupitt, *The Sea of Faith* (BBC Publications 1984).
2 D. Cupitt, *Only Human* (SCM Press 1985).
3 D. Cupitt, *Taking Leave of God* (SCM Press 1980).
4 D. Cupitt, *The World to Come* (SCM Press 1982).

1 CHRISTIAN BELIEF IN GOD

1 See, for example, J. H. Randall, *The Role of Knowledge in Western Religion* (Boston 1958); T. R. Miles, *Religion and the Scientific Outlook* (Allen & Unwin 1959); P. van Buren, *The Secular Meaning of the Gospel* (SCM Press 1963); T. J. J. Altizer and W. Hamilton, *The Death of God* (Penguin 1968).
2 To be found in the *Summa Theologiae*, 1a, 2, 3. The first three of St Thomas's five ways constitute the 'cosmological' argument; the fourth hints at the 'axiological' argument; the fifth is a version of the 'teleological' argument. All these will be explored and defended in chapter 5.

2 THE EBBING OF THEISTIC FAITH

1 See chapter 5, below.
2 Cupitt, *Sea of Faith*, pp. 47f.
3 See, for example, H. Montefiore, *The Probability of God* (SCM Press 1985), ch. 7.
4 A. M. Farrer, *A Science of God?* (Geoffrey Bles 1966), p. 90.
5 See p. 90, below.
6 Cupitt, *Sea of Faith*, pp. 66f.
7 *Ibid.*, pp. 69f.
8 In chapter 6, below.
9 See G. W. F. Hegel, *Early Theological Writings*, tr. T. M. Knox (University of Pennsylvania Press 1971).

10 See K. Barth, *Church Dogmatics*, III. 2 (Eng. trans., T. & T. Clark 1960), pp. 231–42.
11 As, for example, W. & L. Pelz, *God is No More* (Gollancz 1963).
12 In Cupitt, *Sea of Faith*, pp. 209ff.
13 See chapter 6, below.

3 THE INTERIORISATION OF FAITH

1 See chapter 6, below.
2 The work of these philosophers of religion will be considered in chapters 4 and 6.
3 See the early works by Hegel cited in chapter 2, note 10, and J. Fichte, *Attempt at a Critique of All Revelation* (Eng. trans., Cambridge University Press 1978).
4 See A. M. Farrer, *Faith and Speculation* (A. & C. Black 1967).
5 Cupitt, *Sea of Faith*, p. 54.
6 *Ibid*.
7 J. H. Newman, *An Essay in Aid of a Grammar of Assent* (1870, many editions).
8 J. Bowker, *The Sense of God* (Oxford University Press 1973).
9 A. Schweitzer, *Quest of the Historical Jesus* (Eng. trans., Adam & Charles Black 1910, third edn., 1954).
10 A. Schweitzer, *Christianity and the Religions of the World* (Allen & Unwin 1923).
11 S. R. Sutherland, *Faith and Ambiguity* (SCM Press 1984), p. 63.
12 See F. Kerr, *Theology after Wittgenstein* (Basil Blackwell 1986).
13 L. Wittgenstein, *Tractatus Logico-Philosophicus* (Routledge and Kegan Paul 1922).
14 L. Wittgenstein, *Philosophical Investigations* (Basil Blackwell 1953).
15 One thinks particularly of the work of Professors P. T. Geach and G. E. M. Anscombe in this connection.

4 THEISM IN THE MODERN WORLD

1 See, for example, R. Bultmann, *Jesus and the Word* (Eng. trans., Charles Scribner's Sons 1934).

2 See, for example, K. Barth, *Evangelical Theology: an Introduction* (Eng. trans., Weidenfeld & Nicolson 1963).

3 See G. Bornkamm, *Jesus of Nazareth* (Eng. trans., Hodder and Stoughton 1960); E. Käsemann, *Jesus Means Freedom* (Eng. trans., SCM Press 1969); G. Ebeling, *Theology and Proclamation* (Eng. trans., Collins 1966).

4 See the essays collected together in T. F. Torrance, *Transformation and Convergence in the Frame of Knowledge* (Christian Journals 1984).

5 See H. Gollwitzer, *Die Existenz Gottes im Bekenntnis des Glaubens* (Munich 1963).

6 W. Pannenberg, *Theology and the Philosophy of Science* (Eng., trans., Darton Longman & Todd 1976).

7 J. Moltmann, *The Trinity and the Kingdom of God* (Eng. trans., SCM Press 1981).

8 J. Moltmann, *God in Creation* (Eng. trans., SCM Press 1985).

9 E. Jüngel, *God as the Mystery of the World* (Eng. trans., T. & T. Clark 1983).

10 P. Teilhard de Chardin, *The Phenomenon of Man* (Eng. trans., Collins 1959).

11 B. Lonergan, *Insight* (Longmans 1957).

12 B. Lonergan, *Method in Theology* (Darton Longman & Todd 1972).

13 See, for example, K. Rahner, *Foundations of Christian Faith* (Eng. trans., Darton Longman & Todd 1978).

14 H. Küng, *On Being a Christian* (Eng. trans., Collins 1977).

15 H. Küng, *Does God Exist?* (Eng. trans., Collins 1980).

16 J. B. Cobb, *A Christian Natural Theology* (Lutterworth 1966).

17 S. Ogden, *The Reality of God* (Harper 1977).

18 E. Mascall, *He Who Is* (Longmans 1943).

19 E. Mascall, *Christian Theology and Natural Science* (Longmans 1956).

20 A. Farrer, *Finite and Infinite* (Dacre 1947).

21 A. Farrer, *Faith and Speculation* (A. & C. Black 1967).

22 A Farrer, *A Science of God* (Geoffrey Bles 1966).

23 J. Macquarrie, *Principles of Christian Theology* (SCM Press 1966).

24 J. Macquarrie *In Search of Humanity* (SCM Press 1982).

25 J. Macquarrie, *In Search of Deity* (SCM Press 1984).

26 D. Jenkins, *Guide to the Debate about God* (Lutterworth 1966).

27 D. Jenkins, *Living with Questions* (SCM Press 1969).

28 D. Jenkins, *The Glory of Man* (SCM Press 1967).

29 D. Jenkins, *The Contradiction of Christianity* (SCM Press 1976).

30 J. Robinson, *Honest to God* (SCM Press 1963).

31 J. Robinson, *Exploration into God* (SCM Press 1967).

32 See B. Hebblethwaite, *The Incarnation. Collected Essays in Christology* (Cambridge University Press 1987) and 'Providence and divine action', *Religious Studies* (June 1978).

33 M. Wiles, *Faith and the Mystery of God* (Oxford University Press 1984).

34 N. Wolterstorff, *Reason Within the Bounds of Religion* (Eerdmans 1976, 1984).

35 C. F. Delaney, ed., *Rationality and Religious Belief* (Notre Dame 1979).

36 A. Plantinga and N. Wolterstorff, eds., *Faith and Rationality* (Notre Dame 1983).

37 A. Plantinga, *God, Freedom and Evil* (Allen & Unwin 1975).

38 G. Mavrodes, *Belief in God* (University Press of American 1970).

39 M. Goulder and J. H. Hick, *Why Believe in God?* (SCM Press 1983).

40 B. Mitchell, *The Justification of Religious Belief* (Macmillan 1973).

41 R. Swinburne, *The Existence of God* (Oxford University Press 1979).

42 R. Swinburne, *The Coherence of Theism* (Oxford University Press 1977).

43 K. Ward, *Rational Theology and the Creativity of God* (Basil Blackwell 1982).

44 A. Peacocke, *Creation and the World of Science* (Oxford University Press 1979).

45 A. Peacocke, *Intimations of Reality* (Notre Dame 1984).

5 THE SIGNIFICANCE OF KANT

1 Kant, *Critique of Pure Reason* (1781, many editions), Transcendental Doctrine of Elements, First part, Transcendental Aesthetic.

2 B. Magee, *The Philosophy of Schopenhauer* (Oxford University Press 1983), p. 119.

3 Unity, plurality, totality, reality, negation, limitation, substance, causality, reciprocity, possibility, existence,

necessity. See *Critique of Pure Reason*, Transcendental Analytic, book I, chapter I, section 3.

4 Kant, *Critique of Practical Reason* (1788, many editions), part I, book II, chapter II.

5 A. Schopenhauer, *The World as Will and Representation* (1818, many editions), ch. 39.

6 R. Otto, *The Idea of the Holy* (Eng. trans., Oxford University Press 1923).

7 See above, pp. 58ff.

8 G. Berkeley, *Three Dialogues between Hylas and Philonous* (1713, many editions).

9 See F. C. Copleston, *A History of Philosophy*, vol. VII, part II (Doubleday 1965), p. 183.

10 J.-P. Sartre, *Being and Nothingness* (Eng. trans., Methuen 1957), part IV.

11 See V. Descombes, *Modern French Philosophy* (Eng. trans., Cambridge University Press 1981).

6 THE GROUNDS OF THEISTIC BELIEF

1 D. Hume, *Dialogues Concerning Natural Religion* (1779, many editions), part XI.

2 See B. Hebblethwaite, *Evil, Suffering and Religion* (Sheldon Press 1976).

3 From the Greek word *axia* meaning worth or value.

4 These expressions 'bottom-up' and 'top-down' are popularised in the writings of J. R. Searle (see his *Minds, Brains and Science*, BBC Publications 1984), in order to bring out the contrast between explanations in terms of the basic stuff out of which human beings are made, and explanations in terms of the highest end-product of evolution, namely, mind. 'Final' causes are precisely such intended goals.

5 Hume, *Natural Religion*, part II.

6 J. Bowker, *The Sense of God* (Oxford University Press 1973).

7 J. L. Mackie, *The Miracle of Theism* (Oxford University Press 1982).

8 *Ibid.*, p. 141.

9 *Ibid.*, p. 118.

10 *Ibid.*, p.163.

11 See. F. R. Tennant, *Philosophical Theology*, vol. II (Cambridge University Press 1937), and J. H. Hick, *Evil and the God of Love* (Macmillan 1966).

7 THE QUESTION OF TRUTH

1 See J. Derrida, *Writing and Difference* (Eng. trans., Routledge & Kegan Paul 1978).

2 On these ideas see W. V. O. Quine, *Ontological Relativity* (Columbia University Press 1969) and S. P. Schwartz, ed., *Naming, Necessity, and Natural Kinds* (Cornell University Press 1977).

3 A. Quinton, *The Nature of Things* (Routlege & Kegan Paul 1973).

4 M. Devitt, *Realism and Truth* (Basil Blackwell 1984).

5 See. K. Popper, *Objective Knowledge* (Oxford University Press 1972). Popper calls material objects 'World 1', human minds 'World 2' and the cultural products of human minds 'World 3'.

6 See chapter 6, note 4.

7 See pp. 55f., above.

8 See p. 84.

8 RELIGIONS – THEISTIC AND NON-THEISTIC

1 See W. M. Abbott, ed., *The Documents of Vatican II* (Chapman 1966), pp. 656–71.

2 P. Berger, *The Social Reality of Religion* (Faber 1969, Penguin 1973), p. 37.

3 P. Tillich, *Christianity and the Encounter of the World Religions* (Columbia University Press 1963), ch. 1.

4 J. H. Hick, *God and the Universe of Faiths* (Macmillan 1973, Fontana 1976), p. 140.

5 See above, p. 77.

6 M. Eliade, 'The true dreams of mankind: a conversation', *Encounter* (March 1980).

7 See above, pp. 45f.

8 E. Troeltsch, *Christian Thought* (University of London Press 1923), p. 32.

9 See J. H. Hick, *Problems of Religious Pluralism* (Macmillan 1985).

10 See above, p. 56.

11 W. Pannenberg, 'Towards a theology of the history of religions', reprinted in *Basic Questions in Theology*, vol. II (SCM Press 1971).

12 I have endeavoured to expound and defend the Christian doctrine of the Incarnation in a number of essays collected together in the volume referred to in chapter 4, note 32.

13 See B. Hebblethwaite, *The Christian Hope* (Marshall Morgan & Scott 1984), pp. 218–20.

9 LIFE AFTER DEATH

1 A. M. Farrer, *Saving Belief* (Hodder & Stoughton 1964), p. 141.
2 J. H. Hick, 'Eschatological verification reconsidered', *Religious Studies*, 1977, reprinted in *Problems of Religious Pluralism* (Macmillan 1985).
3 I. T. Ramsey, *Models and Mystery* (Oxford University Press, 1964), p. 17.
4 Teilhard de Chardin, *Phenomenon of Man*, book III, chs. 1 and 2.
5 Nietzsche, *Thus Spoke Zarathustra* (1891/2, many editions), part III.
6 P. Berger, *A Rumour of Angels* (Penguin 1970), pp. 70ff.
7 J. H. Hick, *Death and Eternal Life* (Collins 1976), ch. 3.
8 See C. C. J. Webb, *God and Personality* (Allen & Unwin 1919).
9 The Wisdom of Solomon 3.1.
10 Mark 12.27 and parallels.
11 See chapter 8, note 13.
12 See B. Hebblethwaite, *Evil, Suffering and Religion* (Sheldon Press 1976).
13 Cupitt, *Sea of Faith*, p. 33.

10 THE CHRISTIAN CHURCH AND OBJECTIVE THEISM

1 See above, pp. 67f.
2 Macquarrie, *In Search of Deity*.
3 See above, pp. 61f.
4 John 8.32.
5 Romans 8.26.
6 E.g., W. Kasper, *The God of Jesus Christ* (Eng. trans., SCM Press 1984), and J. Moltmann, *The Trinity and the Kingdom of God* (Eng. trans., SCM Press 1981).

Appendix THE CHURCH'S MINISTRY

1 S. W. Sykes, *The Identity of Christianity* (SPCK 1984), ch. 1.
2 L. Wittgenstein, *Philosophical Investigations* (Basil Blackwell 1958), p. 32.
3 See *Karl Barth–Rudolf Bultmann, Briefwechsel 1922–1966* (Theologische Verlag, Zurich 1971), pp. 279–97.

Select bibliography

1 CHRISTIAN BELIEF IN GOD

Smart, N., *The Phenomenon of Christianity* (Collins 1979).
Macquarrie, J., *The Faith of the People of God* (SCM Press 1972).
Farrer, A. M., *Saving Belief* (Hodder & Stoughton 1964).

2 THE EBBING OF THEISTIC FAITH

Cupitt, D., *The Sea of Faith* (BBC 1984).
Chadwick, O., *The Secularisation of the European Mind in the Nineteenth Century* (Cambridge University Press 1975).

3 THE INTERIORISATION OF FAITH

Cupitt, D., *Only Human* (SCM Press 1985); *Life Lines* (SCM Press 1986).
Jennings, T. W., Jr, *Beyond Theism* (Oxford University Press 1985).

4 THEISM IN THE MODERN WORLD

Brown, D., *The Divine Trinity* (Duckworth 1985).
Zahrnt, H., *The Question of God* (Collins 1969).

5 THE SIGNIFICANCE OF KANT

Wood, A. W., *Kant's Rational Theology* (Cornell 1978).
Gunton, C., *Enlightenment and Alienation* (Marshall Morgan & Scott 1985).

6 THE GROUNDS OF THEISTIC BELIEF

Mitchell, B., *The Justification of Religious Belief* (Macmillan 1973).

Select bibliography

Swinburne, R. G., *The Existence of God* (Oxford University Press 1979).

Goulder, M., and Hick, J., *Why Believe in God?* (SCM Press 1983).

7 THE QUESTION OF TRUTH

Christian, W. A., *Meaning and Truth in Religion* (Princeton 1964).

Smart, N., *Philosophers and Religious Truth* (SCM Press 1964).

8 RELIGIONS – THEISTIC AND NON-THEISTIC

Bowker, J., *The Religious Imagination and the Sense of God* (Oxford University Press 1978).

D'Costa, G., *Theology and Religious Pluralism* (Basil Blackwell 1986).

9 LIFE AFTER DEATH

Badham, P., *Christian Beliefs about Life after Death* (Macmillan 1976).

Hebblethwaite, B. L., *The Christian Hope* (Marshall Morgan & Scott 1984).

10 THE CHRISTIAN CHURCH AND OBJECTIVE THEISM

Wiles, M., *Faith and the Mystery of God* (SCM Press 1982).

Sykes, S. W., *The Identity of Christianity* (SPCK 1984).

Quick, O. C., *Doctrines of the Creed* (Nisbet 1938).

Index

Index

Index

DATE DUE